MUSTN'
GRANNY
NETTLES

200 French Expressions

Written by Clare Jones

Illustrated by Tamsin Edwards

Praise for *Mustn't Push Granny in the Nettles: 200 French Expressions*

"Clare Jones's *Mustn't Push Granny in the Nettles* is a cheerful and informative guide to idiomatic and figurative expressions which become hilarious when you try to translate them literally. Organized in useful sections such as food and drink, love, sport or health and happiness, the entries and their charming illustrations constitute a quirky way for any French learner to expand their vocabulary while having a lot of fun. The multiple-choice quizzes at the end of each section add up some interactive entertainment and will be a delight for individuals and groups alike to play and test their knowledge. The book is also a wealth of cultural information and original facts about the origins of some of these idioms and, as such, will also be of interest to native speakers, French learners of English and anybody more generally interested in the oddities of translation. As a lecturer in French and Francophone Studies and Senior Fellow of the Higher Education Academy, I can vouch for the thorough research work that has been carried out for the completion of this book and can anticipate a lot of interest in its future readership."

Dr Marion Krauthaker, Lecturer in French and Francophone Studies, Head of French, School of Arts, University of Leicester.

"I like the drills in your book. It is great fun and highly entertaining."

Dr Michael Abecassis of the University of Oxford Language Centre, 12 Woodstock Road Oxford OX2 6HT England

Cambria and Arial fonts used with permission from Microsoft.

Copyright © 2020 Clare Jones

All rights reserved.

ISBN: 9798624943773

Printed by KDP, An Amazon.com Company

CONTENTS

Preface 7

Introduction 8

1 **Manger et boire** – eating and drinking 9

   Quiz 1 21

   Answers 1 25

2 **Manger et boire (suite)** – eating and drinking (cont.) 26

   L'alcool – alcohol 30

   Quiz 2 40

   Answers 2 44

3 **Apprécier la vie** – enjoying life 45

   Quiz 3 56

   Answers 3 60

4 **Les rires** – laughter 61

   Le bonheur – happiness 66

   La bonne santé – good health 69

   Quiz 4 75

   Answers 4 79

5 **La négativité** – negativity 80

   Les maladies et la physiologie – illnesses and physiology 93

Quiz 5 96

Answers 5 100

6 **Les maladies et la physiologie (suite)** – illnesses and physiology (cont.) 101

Quiz 6 114

Answers 6 118

7 **Les maladies et la physiologie (suite)** – illnesses and physiology (cont.) 119

Le sommeil – sleep 125

La mort – death 129

Quiz 7 132

Answers 7 136

8 **La mort (suite)** – death (cont.) 137

La chance – luck 141

Le sport – sport 143

Quiz 8 151

Answers 8 155

9 **L'attirance et l'apparence** – attraction and appearance 156

Quiz 9 170

Answers 9 174

10 **L'amour, le mariage et l'amitié** – love, marriage and friendship 175

Quiz 10 190

Answers 10   194

Afterword   195

Complete list of expressions   196

More about the author   214

More about the illustrator   215

By the same author and illustrator 216

Bibliography   217

Websites   219

Index 222

Preface

Much of the fun of learning a new language comes after you have learned basic vocabulary and grammatical structures. The real fun starts when you begin to learn and enjoy the figurative expressions used by native speakers. It is often hard to understand the punchline of a joke, the plays on words which make adverts funny, and the resonances in poems and book titles if you do not understand idioms commonly used and understood by most francophones. In this book (which has been evolving for more than a decade) I have brought together 200 of the most common expressions which we might need in general conversation between family and friends. I have added some information about their origins (my sources are mainly Alain Rey, Georges Planelles and Claude Duneton). There are cultural references to show how the expressions have been used in books, plays, films, songs and advertisements. There are also fun quizzes to test your new-found knowledge and to help you judge your progress. Many thanks to Tamsin Edwards for adding humorous illustrations to make the expressions more memorable.

Much of my research has been carried out through decades of notetaking when reading (mainly modern) French novels, newspapers, internet articles and French blogs, but it has been human contacts which have been the main driving force. This book would never have been written without the sound advice and endless patience of my French friends. My conversations and my long correspondence with them have provided me with much material for this book. I would like to thank Florence Pierrard, Marie-Agnès Roussot (forty years of friendship and counting!), Christian Voleau, Michel Meslin, Blandine Schmitt-Monin and Juliette Schmitt for making sure that the French I have used sounds natural to French ears, young and old, and by offering their wisdom and cultural advice. Catherine Pettet, Julie Bedster and Hattie Hammond-Chambers have also been of immense help and have given much encouragement.

Introduction

This is a book about French expressions but what do I mean by an expression? I have used the term in its broadest sense to mean any phrase in common use. You might start a conversation with a simple expression such as '*Ça va ?*', '*Quoi de neuf ?*' or '*Quelles nouvelles ?*' These are set phrases which everyone understands and are appropriate to a certain situation (meeting people and opening conversations – How are you? What's new? What news?) and they can be understood literally. There are many idioms in this book. Idioms are expressions which cannot be taken literally, so for example, if you say, '*J'ai l'estomac dans les talons*', you don't really mean that your stomach is in your heels. All idioms are also expressions but not all expressions are idioms. One or two proverbs have been included too, such as *mieux vaut prévenir que guérir* – 'prevention is better than cure'. Proverbs are truths or words of wisdom which have been passed down through the years, and we still like to use them occasionally.

Not all the expressions in this book are appropriate to use in all situations. Choose carefully! I have used asterisks to show levels of informality or vulgarity to help you to get the tone of a conversation right.

No asterisk = safe to use in any situation
* = colloquial but acceptable in polite circles
** = very colloquial, use with care
*** = vulgar, not to be used in polite society or in professional situations. Beware, vulgar expressions often sound very strange coming out of the mouths of foreigners!

Amuse-toi bien!

CHAPTER 1

Manger et boire – eating and drinking

I like nothing more when I stay with friends in France than to hear the words '*À table !*' It is not only the anticipation of delicious food which excites me, but also that of good conversation, lively discussion and the chance to relax with friends. The French love to argue and philosophise over a lengthy meal! Did you know that an hour and a quarter after French teenagers enter the examination hall to face the *baccalauréat* philosophy paper in June each year, the government releases the questions to the public and they are announced on radio and television and are discussed in the newspapers? Plenty of food for thought at the dinner table too, no doubt!

- ***avoir* ou *crever la dalle*****
  – to be starving hungry

Literally: to have *or* to burst the paving stone

Bon, allez tout le monde ! Cherchons un resto ! On crève la dalle !

Right, come on, you lot! Let's look for a restaurant. We're starving!

You might think that this is a simple metaphor: that you could eat anything, no matter how inedible, because you are so hungry, but no! The modern meaning of *une dalle* is 'a paving stone'. However, its original meaning was 'a stone in which a groove has been cut which is used as a drain'. From this idea came the slang word *dalle* meaning 'the throat' and from here there is only a short step to 'hunger'.

ⓘ The verb *crever* means 'to puncture' or 'to burst' but is frequently used informally to mean 'to die'. You can say, '*Je crève* de faim*' or '*je crève* la faim*' meaning 'I'm starving'. *Un crève-la-faim** is a starving person.

- ***avoir l'estomac dans les talons*** – to be famished *or* starving

Literally: to have the stomach in the heels

Quand est-ce qu'on dîne ? Je commence à avoir l'estomac dans les talons !

When are we eating? I'm starting to get really hungry!

- ***avoir les crocs*** – to be famished *or* starving

Literally: to have the fangs

Qu'est-ce qu'il y a à manger ? J'ai les crocs !

What is there to eat? I'm starving!

ⓘ **Pronunciation point**→ *crocs* rhymes with *eau*.

- ***avoir un bon coup de fourchette*** – to have a hearty appetite

Literally: to have a good blow of fork

Tatie Safia a un bon coup de fourchette. Elle mange toujours plus que moi.

Auntie Safia has a hearty appetite. She always eats more than me.

- ***avoir un petit creux*** – to feel a little hungry

Literally: to have a little hollow

*« Un petit sablé avec ton café ?
– Ah oui, je veux bien ! J'ai un petit creux. »*

'A shortbread biscuit with your coffee?'
'Ah, yes, please! I do feel a little hungry.'

- ***avoir une faim de loup*** – to be as hungry as a wolf

Literally: to have a hunger of wolf

En rentrant de notre randonnée en montagne, on avait une faim de loup et on s'est précipités vers une pâtisserie.

Coming back from our mountain hike, we were hungry as wolves and dived into a cake shop.

- **boire à sa soif ; manger à sa faim** – to satisfy one's thirst; to eat one's fill

Literally: to drink to one's thirst; to eat to one's hunger

Ne soyez pas timides ! Mangez à votre faim ! Il y en a bien assez pour tout le monde.

Don't be shy! Eat your fill! There's plenty to go around!

- Also: **boire jusqu'à plus soif** – to quench one's thirst; to drink one's fill; to drink all one can

Literally: to drink until no more thirst

Après deux heures de footing, j'ai été soulagé de pouvoir boire jusqu'à plus soif.

After two hours of jogging, I was relieved to be able to quench my thirst.

(i) *Jusqu'à plus soif* can also be used figuratively to mean 'till one can't take any more; to one's heart's content'. '*Je pourrais citer des exemples jusqu'à plus soif*' – 'I could keep quoting examples to your heart's content'.

- ***Bon appétit !*** – enjoy your meal!

Literally: good appetite

Et voici votre pizza trois fromages, monsieur. Bon appétit !

And here's your three-cheese pizza, sir. Enjoy your meal!

❗ Though this expression is widely used in France and has been taken to heart by many English people, some schools of good manners would advise against its use. It could be argued that dinner parties are occasions to focus upon the good company and conversation, and that one should not draw attention to the bestial side of the meal.

- ***c'est du jus de chaussette*** – it's like dishwater

Literally: it is sock juice

Ce café soluble est dégoûtant. C'est du jus de chaussette.

This instant coffee is disgusting. It's like dishwater.

📝 According to the *Revue Lorraine Populaire,* in times gone by, socks were used to filter coffee when no better filter was available. There's no saying they were clean!

- ***c'est mon péché mignon*** – it's my guilty pleasure; it's my (little) weakness; I have a weakness for it

Literally: it's my cute sin

J'aime prendre un carré de chocolat avec mon café. C'est mon péché mignon.

I like to have a piece of chocolate with my coffee. It's my guilty pleasure.

- ***ce n'est pas de refus*** * – I wouldn't say no

Literally: it is not of refusal

« *Un peu de vin, Louis ?*
— *Ce n'est pas de refus.* »

'A little wine, Louis?'
'I wouldn't say no.'

- ***croquer*** ou ***dévorer*** ou ***mordre quelque chose à belles dents*** – to wolf something down

Literally: to crunch *or* devour *or* bite into something with beautiful teeth

Quand le jeune SDF est arrivé au resto du cœur, il a croqué son pain à belles dents.

When the young homeless boy arrived at the soup kitchen, he wolfed down his bread.

This expression dates from around the 15th century. *Belles* can be translated as 'large' as in the expression *avoir un bel appétit.* The expression obviously refers to the large teeth of a wild animal – *un croc* is 'a fang' and the verb *croquer* is 'to bite into' or 'to crunch'.

- **déjeuner sur le pouce*** – to have a quick snack

Literally: to lunch on the thumb

Après avoir déjeuné sur le pouce, j'ai pu passer le reste de la pause de midi à faire du lèche-vitrines.

After having a quick snack, I was able to spend the rest of the lunch break window-shopping.

Un pouce as well as being 'a thumb' is also 'an inch'. Being a measurement of something small, it is used in this expression to mean 'a short amount of time'. Also, if you are having a quick snack, you are most likely eating with your fingers and thumbs.

- **dîner à la bonne franquette** *– to have an informal *or* pot luck dinner

Literally: no real literal translation – to dine in the good 'straightforwardness' style

Venez dîner chez nous ! Ce sera à la bonne franquette.

Come and eat with us! It will be pot luck.

If someone invites you to dine with them *à la bonne franquette*, it probably means that they are not going to go to a lot of trouble preparing a sumptuous meal for you. *Un dîner à la bonne franquette* can also be a meal where each guest brings along a dish, so it would be best to clarify this before setting off for dinner just in case you are expected to provide food!

- **entre la poire et le fromage** – during a quiet, relaxed moment between two events

Literally: between the pear and the cheese

Entre la poire et le fromage, Edwige m'a confié qu'elle allait quitter son mari.

Quite casually over dinner, Edwige confided in me that she was going to leave her husband.

Whereas it is now considered normal in France to serve cheese followed by fruit or a dessert, in the 17th century when this expression first developed, the fruit (a pear or maybe an apple) came first. Towards the end of a convivial meal, there comes a point when guests relax and conversation flows, and this is the moment *entre la poire et le fromage* when secrets might be told, or perhaps juicy bits of gossip might be shared. However, the meaning of the expression has generalised and can refer to a quiet, relaxed moment between any two events, and not necessarily at a dinner table.

- **faire la fine bouche** – to be picky; to turn one's nose up at things which are generally appreciated

Literally: to make the fine mouth

Je n'aime pas inviter Jean-Louis à dîner parce qu'il fait toujours la fine bouche.

I don't like to invite Jean-Louis to dinner because he's always so picky.

This expression has been around since the 15th century. It started out as *faire la petite bouche*. It is easy to imagine someone with a large mouth swallowing lots of good food with great gusto. The opposite would be someone who makes a small mouth in order to reject what is on offer. The expression evolved over the years, *petite* changing to *fine,* and the meaning expanding to include turning one's nose up at anything normally considered good.

- ***je n'en peux plus*** – I'm full

Literally: I can't of it anymore

*« Et pour finir, mes amis, voici les truffes au chocolat à la liqueur de prunes.
– Vraiment, Florence, je n'en peux plus! »*

'And to finish, my friends, here are the chocolate truffles with plum liqueur.'
'Really, Florence, I'm full!'

Be careful not to fall into the trap of translating 'I'm full' literally into French. *Je suis plein(e)** can mean 'I am drunk'. Also, when a cow or other female animal is pregnant, she is *pleine*, so if a woman says, '*Je suis pleine*', holding her full stomach, she is likely to have her French host falling into a fit of giggles!

- ***l'appétit vient en mangeant (proverbe)*** – eating whets the appetite; (figuratively) the more you have, the more you want

Literally: the appetite comes by eating

Mamie a été malade, et elle a perdu du poids. J'ai essayé de l'encourager à manger en lui préparant une soupe savoureuse et en lui disant que l'appétit vient en mangeant.

Granny has been ill, and she has lost weight. I tried to encourage her to eat by preparing her a delicious soup and by telling her that eating whets the appetite.

And figuratively:

L'année dernière, j'ai offert à ma grand-mère son premier téléphone mobile tout simple. Comme l'appétit vient en mangeant, pour Noël cette année, elle voudrait un smartphone dernier cri.

Last year, I gave my grandmother her first simple mobile phone. As the more you have, the more you want, for Christmas this year, she'd like a state-of-the-art smartphone.

Rabelais used this proverb in his 16th century work *Gargantua* which tells the story of a giant with a monstrous appetite. The origin might well be much more ancient, however, going back to classical literature.

- ***manger comme quatre*** – to eat like a horse

Literally: to eat like four

Après une heure au gymnase, j'étais tellement affamée que j'ai mangé comme quatre !

After an hour at the gym, I was so starving hungry, I ate like a horse!

- ***manger** ou **dévorer comme un ogre*** – to eat like a horse

Literally: to eat *or* devour like an ogre

Mon petit chiot mange comme un ogre. Il va être énorme !

My little puppy eats like a horse. He's going to be enormous!

Quiz 1

1. *J'aime prendre un petit cognac comme digestif. C'est mon péché …*
a) *mignon.*
b) *malin.*
c) *vénal.*

2. *« Encore un morceau de gâteau, Maxence ?*
– Merci, Diane, … »
a) *je n'en ai plus.*
b) *je n'en peux plus.*
c) *je ne peux non plus.*

3. *Il aime manger. Il a un bon coup de …*
a) *cuillère.*
b) *couteau.*
c) *fourchette.*

4. *Elle m'a dit cela entre …*
a) *le fromage et la poire.*
b) *la poire et le fromage.*
c) *une poire et du fromage.*

5. *Denis est passé nous voir à l'improviste hier soir. On a dîné à la bonne …*
a) *franchise.*
b) *française.*
c) *franquette.*

6. *Un coq au vin pour madame et un bœuf bourguignon pour monsieur. Voilà ! ...*
a) *Bonne journée !*
b) *Bon appétit !*
c) *Bonne continuation !*

7. *Elle a un très grand appétit. Elle mange comme ...*
a) *quatorze.*
b) *quatre.*
c) *quarante.*

8. *Ils sont si pauvres qu'ils ne mangent jamais ... leur faim.*
a) *de*
b) *en*
c) *à*

9. *La tarte aux pommes de ma belle-mère était si bonne que nous l'avons dévorée à ... dents.*
a) *grandes*
b) *jolies*
c) *belles*

10. *Après une heure de musculation, j'ai toujours l'estomac dans les ...*
a) *chevilles.*
b) *orteils.*
c) *talons.*

11. *D'habitude je ne mange pas à l'heure du goûter, mais cet après-midi j'ai ...*
a) *un petit creux.*
b) *le Creuset.*
c) *une petite croix.*

12. « Une bière, Nathan ?
– Ce n'est pas de … »
a) non.
b) refuge.
c) refus.

13. Je ne veux pas qu'il dîne chez nous. Il fait toujours la… bouche et je ne sais jamais comment le nourrir.
a) fine
b) grande
c) longue

14. Je veux manger tout de suite. Je crève la …
a) dalle.
b) balle.
c) halle.

15. Je n'ai pas eu le temps d'aller au restaurant. J'ai dû déjeuner sur …
a) le pouce.
b) le majeur.
c) l'index.

16. Je n'ai pas eu le temps de manger à midi et maintenant j'ai les …
a) rots.
b) eaux.
c) crocs.

17. Il a un énorme appétit. Il mange comme …
a) un ogre.
b) un géant.
c) un lutin.

18. J'espère qu'il y a quelque chose de consistant à manger. J'ai une faim de …
a) *renard.*
b) *loup.*
c) *blaireau.*

19. *Ce café n'a aucun arôme. C'est du jus de …*
a) *bas.*
b) *chaussette.*
c) *linge.*

20. *Il a commencé par voler de vieilles voitures, mais l'appétit vient … et maintenant ce sont des Mercedes neuves dont il a envie.*
a) *en cuisant*
b) *en mangeant*
c) *en buvant*

Answers 1

1. a   11. a
2. b   12. c
3. c   13. a
4. b   14. a
5. c   15. a
6. b   16. c
7. b   17. a
8. c   18. b
9. c   19. b
10. c 20. b

CHAPTER 2

Manger et boire (suite) – eating and drinking (cont.)

Although the emergence of *les fast foods* (or to give it its proper French name, *'la restauration rapide'*) has changed French eating habits for the worse recently, the French are still much more likely than the English to take a long lunch break and to return home for a proper family meal around the table at midday. It is still common to find shops and businesses closed for two hours for lunch.

A 2015 poll discovered, not surprisingly, that the French spent more time per day eating and drinking than any other OECD nation. At 2 hours and 13 minutes, they spent more than twice as long over their food and drink than the Americans, who devoted only one hour and 2 minutes to eating and drinking (the quickest eaters in the survey of 29 countries). The UK was in a poor twentieth place with one hour and 18 minutes given over to food and drink.

- ***manger du bout des dents*** – to pick at one's food

Literally: to eat from the end of the teeth

Ce plat était nouveau pour elle ; elle l'a mangé du bout des dents.

This dish was new to her; she picked at it.

- ***mettre les petits plats dans les grands*** – to lay on a first-rate meal; to go to great effort or expense to please somebody

Literally: to put the little dishes in the big ones

Il faut faire notre possible pour plaire à ma nouvelle patronne. Mettons les petits plats dans les grands, et un jour nous serons récompensés, j'en suis sûr !

We must do our utmost to please my new boss. Let's put on a first-rate meal, and one day we will be rewarded, I'm sure!

This expression dates from the 19th century. *Les petits plats* are dishes prepared with great care, and *les grands plats* are quite simply large plates. A meal where *les petit plats* are put in *les grands* would be a meal where delicious dishes are served in great quantity.

(i) The expression can be used figuratively in the sense of 'to go to great effort or expense' and does not have to have anything to do with food.

- ***mieux vaut l'avoir en photo qu'à (sa) table*** ou ***qu'en vacances*** ou ***qu'en pension*** – he'll *or* she'll eat you (/us, etc.) out of house and home

Literally: better to have him *or* her in a photo than at (one's) table *or* on holiday *or* boarding

« *Tu n'as pas oublié, chéri, que mon cousin Henri dîne chez nous ce soir ? Il faudra faire des courses.*
  – *Ah oui, Henri le gourmand ! Mieux vaut l'avoir en photo qu'à table !* »

'Did you remember, darling, that my cousin Henri is dining with us this evening? We'll have to do some shopping.'
'Oh yes, greedy Henri! He'll eat us out of house and home!'

- **la note est salée*** – the bill is a bit steep

Literally: the bill is salted

Je n'aime pas la nouvelle pizzeria en ville. L'accueil n'est pas chaleureux et la note est salée.

I don't like the new pizzeria in town. They don't give you a warm welcome and they charge a lot.

If you add too much salt to something, it can be a nasty shock to the system. In the 17th century the adjective *salé* took on the figurative meaning of 'exaggerated' which is why the bill is said to be salted.

- ***qui dort dîne (proverbe)*** – he who sleeps forgets his hunger

Literally: who sleeps, dines

Quand Clovis n'avait pas l'argent pour manger à sa faim, il se couchait en se disant : « Qui dort, dîne ».

When Clovis didn't have the money to fill his belly, he would go to bed, telling himself, 'He who sleeps forgets his hunger'.

- ***s'en mettre*** ou ***s'en fourrer jusque là**** – to stuff oneself*; to feed one's face*; to have a slap-up meal*; to have a real blow out*; to have a nosh-up* (UK)

Literally: to put *or* to stuff oneself (of it) up to there

Quel beau repas hier soir ! Je m'en suis mis jusque là !

What a great meal last night! I had a real blow out!

ⓘ In Jacques Offenbach's operetta *La Vie Parisienne*, the Swiss baron Gondremarck is looking forward to stuffing himself during his three-month stay in Paris. He complains that his upbringing has been too austere but that he now intends to make up for this. He sings:

'Je veux m'en fourrer fourrer jusque là !
Je veux m'en fourrer fourrer jusque là !
Portez la lettre à Métella !
Je veux m'en fourrer fourrer jusque là !'

If you do a quick search online, you will be sure to find a video of this song. Beware, it is very catchy, and you'll be singing it all day long!

- ***tenir table ouverte*** – to keep open house

Literally: to hold open table

Venez dîner chez nous n'importe quand. Je tiens toujours table ouverte pour les amis.

Come and dine with us whenever you like. I always keep open house for friends.

- ***vous m'en direz des nouvelles*** – you will like it

Literally: you will tell me some news of it

J'ai préparé des pains au chocolat dont tu me diras des nouvelles. Ils viennent juste de sortir du four.

You're going to like the chocolate pastries I've prepared. They've only just come out of the oven.

L'alcool – alcohol

Binge drinking used to be thought of as a peculiarly British problem, but it does seem that '*le binge drinking*' is on the rise in France, so much so that it has been thought necessary to invent a French phrase to translate the concept: *la beuverie express.*

There are simply too many colourful expressions concerning alcohol to put them all in this book! Here are just a few of them.

- ***À la tienne Étienne !*** * – Cheers!*

Literally: to yours Étienne!

« *Je suis si content de te revoir, Rémi ! Trinquons ! À la tienne Étienne !*
– *À la tienne, mon vieux !* »

'I am so happy to see you, Rémi! Let's have a toast! Cheers!'
'Cheers, mate!'

A bawdy drinking song of 1863 was the source of this expression. The chorus goes: '*À la tienne Étienne / À la tienne, mon vieux ! / Sans ces garc's de femm's / Nous serions tous des frères / À la tienne Étienne, / À la tienne, mon vieux ! / Sans ces garc's de femm's / Nous serions tous heureux !*'

'To you Étienne! / To you, mate! / Without these bitches / we would all be brothers. / To you Étienne! / To you, mate! / Without these bitches / we would all be happy.'

If you do an online search for this refrain, you can easily find a recording to listen to. There was one made by Les Quatre Barbus. Given the misogynistic origin of '*à la tienne Étienne*', you might want to stick to the shorter version '*à la tienne !*' or more formally '*à la vôtre !*' – 'to yours', which has probably been in use since the mid-16th century. This is a variation of '*à ta santé !/à votre santé !*' meaning 'to your health'.

It is important to look into the eyes of your fellow drinkers as your glasses touch. This tradition apparently goes back to the Middle Ages when it was not unknown for a noble to try to slip some poison into his rival's wine. To counter this, everyone clinked glasses so that the wine from one glass might pass into the glass of another. If anyone refused to drink from their glass after a toast, this was an indication that the wine might be poisoned, and no-one would drink. Even if we no longer fear being poisoned, the tradition of looking into the eyes of those with whom we are clinking glasses persists and it can only add to the *bonne ambiance* at the dinner table.

- ***avoir la gueule de bois**** – to have a hangover

Literally: to have the mouth of wood

« Oh là là. J'ai la gueule de bois. Combien de bières est-ce que je me suis enfilé cette nuit ? »

'Ohhh, I've got a hangover. How many beers did I knock back last night?'

(i) The best-selling author Marc Levy extends the metaphor very effectively in his novel *La prochaine fois*:
*– Où es-tu ? demanda-t-il à Peter.
– En enfer ! J'ai une gueule de bois en chêne massif et ma réunion est avancée d'une heure.*
'Where are you?' he asked Peter.
'In hell! I have a massive hangover and my meeting has been brought forward an hour.' ('I have a mouth of wood in solid oak'.)

- ***avoir le vin mauvais** ou **gai** ou **triste*** – *to get nasty* or *happy* or *sad after a few drinks*

Literally: to have the bad *or* gay *or* sad wine

Je buvais beaucoup quand j'étais plus jeune, mais je n'ai jamais eu le vin mauvais. Je devenais plutôt affectueux.

I used to drink a lot when I was younger, but it never made me nasty. Rather I would become affectionate.

This expression has been in use since 1696 but is still current.

Notice the position of the adjective *mauvais* in this expression. There might be two reasons for avoiding the company of a certain person: one might be that he is nasty after a few drinks, *il a le vin mauvais*, and the other might be that he offers bad wine to his guests, *il a du mauvais vin*!

- **avoir un (p'tit) coup dans le nez*** – to have had one too many *or* a drop too much; to be in a very bad way

    Literally: to have a (little) knock in the nose

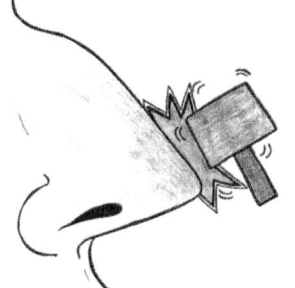

Ne fais pas attention à Nadège. Elle a un p'tit coup dans le nez.

Don't worry about Nadège. She's had a drop too much.

A variation on this expression is:
- **avoir un verre dans le nez*** – to have had one too many *or* a bit too much to drink

Literally: to have a glass in the nose

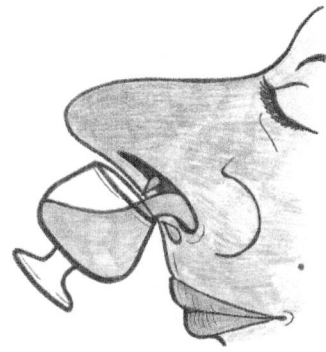

- ***avoir une bonne descente*** * – to be able to really knock it back*

Literally: to have a good descent

Lina a une bonne descente : gin, martini, vin… elle aime tout.

Lina can really knock it back: gin, martini, wine… she likes it all.

- ***boire cul sec*** – to drink down in one

Literally: to drink bottom *or* arse (*Brit*) *or* ass (*US*) dry

Bruno a levé son verre, et glou, glou, glou, il l'a bu cul sec.

Bruno raised his glass, and glug, glug, glug, he drank it down in one.

(i) Notice that this is not a vulgar expression. It can be used in polite society. It simply means to drink until the bottom of the glass (*le cul*) is dry.

- ***ça s'arrose !*** * – let's drink to that; that calls for a drink

Literally: that waters itself

C'est un beau bébé qui respire la santé. Ça s'arrose !

He's a beautiful bouncing baby. That calls for a drink!

- ***être beurré(e) (comme un p'tit Lu)***** – to be sloshed* *or* plastered*

Literally: to be buttered (like a little biscuit)

Alain a passé toute la journée dans le bar et il est rentré beurré comme un p'tit Lu.

Alain spent all day in the bar and came home plastered.

The expression *être beurré* has most likely evolved because *beurré* sounds like *bourré* which also means 'drunk' in French slang. Also, when someone is drunk, their speech slides around in their mouth as if the words were buttered.

The *p'tit Lu* refers to the *petits-beurre* biscuits made since the mid-19th century by the firm Lefèvre-Utile which shortens to LU.

- ***être soûl(e) comme un cochon*** – to be as drunk as a lord

Literally: to be drunk as a pig

C'est une catastrophe ! Le chef de cuisine boit depuis ce matin et il est soûl comme un cochon.

It's a disaster! The chef has been drinking since this morning and he's as drunk as a lord.

ⓘ There are lots of other similes on the theme of drunkenness scattered through French literature but many of them have fallen out of favour. However, you will still sometimes hear **soûl comme un Polonais** – as drunk as a Pole. A racist slur? Well, yes, probably best avoided, but the expression does have an interesting origin (see below), which is why I am including it here. You might prefer to stick to another way of saying someone drinks likes a fish: ***il/elle boit comme un trou*** (he/she drinks like a hole) ***et il/elle est ivre mort*** – and he/she is blind drunk (literally dead drunk), or ***il/elle est plein(e) comme une barrique*** * – he/she is full like a barrel.

Whether this be entirely true or not (and we cannot be sure), it has been suggested by some authors (e.g. Gilles Mathis in *Le cliché*, 1998) that *soûl comme un Polonais* is a back-handed compliment to the Polish nation rather than a xenophobic slur. The story goes that the night before an important battle against the Spaniards in 1808, Napoleon allowed his soldiers to drink to quell their nerves. The following morning, only the Polish mercenaries were in any fit state to fight valiantly, either because they held their drink better than the French, or because they had drunk less. When Napoleon saw the state of his troops, he is thought to have said, '*Si vous voulez vous soûler, soûlez-vous comme les Polonais*' – 'If you want to get drunk, get drunk like the Poles'.

ⓘ You might also have seen the word *soûl(e)* written as either *saoul(e)* (an older form of the word which is still preferred by many writers today) or *soul(e)*. In 1990 l'Académie française made recommendations to modernise French spellings, and words which contained a circumflex accent over the *u* dropped the accent if it would make no difference to their pronunciation by doing so, hence *soûl* would become *soul*. All three versions are acceptable. However, some modern French dictionaries do not list the new spelling. They list the word *soul* uniquely to refer to soul music.

A quick reminder about pronunciation: in the masculine form of the adjective, the final *l* is not pronounced.

- **être rond comme une queue de pelle*** – to be rolling drunk

Literally: to be round as a shovel handle

Le jour de ses vingt-et-un ans, Hugues avait bu trois bouteilles de vin et il était rond comme une queue de pelle.

On his twenty-first birthday, Hugues had drunk three bottles of wine and he was rolling drunk.

People who eat and drink to excess end up with a pot belly and a round shape, hence they are *rond*. Over the course of history, this expression has lost its food association, and just the meaning of 'drunk' has been kept. *Être rond comme...* can be followed by a variety of different objects round in shape such as *une queue de pelle (*if you imagine the shovel handle cut in cross-section) or *une queue de poêle* (a frying pan-handle), *une bille* (a marble), *une balle* (a ball), *une boule* (a ball or bowl), *une pomme* (an apple), *une barrique* (a barrel), *un disque* (a disc, disk, or discus), *un boudin* (a sausage), *une bûche* (a log), *un œuf* (an egg), *une soucoupe* (a saucer), *un zéro* (a zero), or *un petit-pois* (a pea).

- ***prendre une cuite*** ** – to get plastered*; to get sloshed*

Literally: to take a cooked

La dernière fois que j'ai pris une cuite à Marseille, ça ne s'est pas bien terminé et j'ai été malade comme un chien.

The last time I got plastered in Marseilles, it didn't end well, and I was sick as a dog.

Une cuite comes from the verb *cuire,* to cook. *Être cuit* at first meant 'to be cooked', and in the moral sense 'to be ruined', then *il est cuit* took on the meaning still used in colloquial modern French of 'it's all over for him'. In the 17th century it started to be used informally to mean 'drunk'.

We'd better finish this chapter on a more sober note!

- ***se mettre au régime sec*** – to go on the wagon; to stop drinking alcohol

Literally: to put oneself at the dry diet

Ma meilleure copine, Margot, dit qu'elle en a marre de s'enivrer et qu'elle va se mettre au régime sec. On verra bien !

My best mate, Margot, says she's fed up of getting drunk and she's going on the wagon. We'll see!

Quiz 2

1. *Gaspard ne boit plus ; il s'est mis au régime ...*
a) *sac.*
b) *sec.*
c) *sèche.*

2. *Gabriel a une bonne ... , non ? Il a toujours une bière à la main.*
a) *descente.*
b) *détente.*
c) *attente.*

3. *Tu as trente ans aujourd'hui ! Ça ... !*
a) *s'arrose*
b) *arrose*
c) *m'arrose*

4. *A la réception de mariage, le père de la jeune mariée était ... comme une queue de pelle.*
a) *rond*
b) *carré*
c) *ovale*

5. *J'ai trop bu hier soir. J'ai ...*
a) *la gueule de boire.*
b) *la gueule de bois.*
c) *les lèvres de bois.*

6. *Je vous recommande la tarte aux pommes de ma belle-mère. Vous m'en direz …*
a) *des nouveaux.*
b) *des nouvelles.*
c) *une nouvelle.*

7. *Manon s'est couchée sans manger ce soir. En effet, qui dort …*
a) *mange.*
b) *rêve.*
c) *dîne.*

8. *Après avoir bu cinq bières, Thomas était beurré comme…*
a) *un p'tit Loup.*
b) *une petite Loupe.*
c) *un p'tit Lu.*

9. *J'aime bien ton papa mais il est si gourmand, mieux vaut l'avoir … qu'à table.*
 a) *au restaurant*
b) *au bar*
c) *en photo*

10. *« Trinquons au nouveau bébé ! ...*
a) *– À la tienne Ben ! »*
b) *– À la tienne Étienne ! »*
c) *– À la tienne Amen ! »*

11. *Je tiens table… pour les amis.*
a) *offerte*
b) *obligée*
c) *ouverte*

12. *Sylvain a passé la journée au bar. Je crois qu'il a un p'tit coup dans …*
a) *le nez.*
b) *le pied.*
c) *la jambe.*

13. *J'ai comme l'impression que ton papa n'aime pas ma cuisine. Il mange du bout …*
a) *des dents.*
b) *de la langue.*
c) *de la bouche.*

14. *Pour fêter les noces d'or de nos parents nous allons mettre les … dans les grands.*
a) *petites assiettes*
b) *petits plats*
c) *petits bols*

15. *Deux cents euros pour un repas banal ! La note est …*
a) *poivrée.*
b) *salée.*
c) *épicée.*

16. « *Tu as bien mangé hier soir ?*
– *En effet, je m'en suis … jusque là !* »
a) *mû*
b) *misé*
c) *mis*

17. « *Tu as trop bu samedi dernier ?*
– *Oui, j'ai …* »
a) *pris une pomme.*
b) *cuit une pomme.*
c) *pris une cuite.*

18. *Je te déconseille de sortir avec Jean-Luc parce qu'il a …*
a) *le vin mauvais.*
b) *du mauvais vin.*
c) *un vin mauvais.*

19. *Camille avait soif. Elle l'a bu…*
a) *cul sec.*
b) *cul de sac.*
c) *cul sac.*

20. *Yves s'est déjà enfilé six canettes et il est soûl comme …*
a) *un cochon.*
b) *un mouton.*
c) *un chameau.*

Answers 2

1.	b	11.	c
2.	a	12.	a
3.	a	13.	a
4.	a	14.	b
5.	b	15.	b
6.	b	16.	c
7.	c	17.	c
8.	c	18.	a
9.	c	19.	a
10.	b	20.	a

CHAPTER 3

Apprécier la vie – enjoying life

It is sometimes said that the French live more in the moment than people born in English-speaking nations. In the UK we are constantly being told about the benefits of mindfulness. The French have been practising this for a long time! You could say that the most important French verb is *être*, whereas the British and Americans prefer *faire* or *avoir*.

- **à tire-larigot*** – to your heart's content; like there's no tomorrow

Literally: at pull- flute

J'adore les réceptions de mariage. On peut y boire à tire-larigot !

I love wedding receptions. You can drink to your heart's content!

Boire à tyre Larigault was the original form of this 16th century expression. It meant 'to drink bottle after bottle in one go'. The *larigot* was a rustic flute, and there is a link to the verb *flûter* which meant 'to empty glasses' or 'to drink a lot' (perhaps flautists drank a great deal, or the shape of the bottle and the flute were similar; other more baudy origins are also possible). The old word for flute, *larigot*, has fallen from use except in this expression, *à tire-larigot*, which now means 'in great quantity' or 'to your heart's content'. It can be used in contexts other than drinking.

Another possible origin is to do with the bell called *La Rigaud* which was in Rouen cathedral. It might be that the bell ringers had so much trouble getting such a big bell to sound by pulling on the bell rope (the French for 'to pull' is *tirer*), that they became very thirsty and, of course, had to drink a lot, hence *boire à tire-larigot*.

- ***avoir les doigts de pied en éventail*** – to have one's feet up

Literally: to have the toes fanned out

Je croyais qu'il devait travailler mais il avait les doigts de pieds en éventail et il regardait la télé.

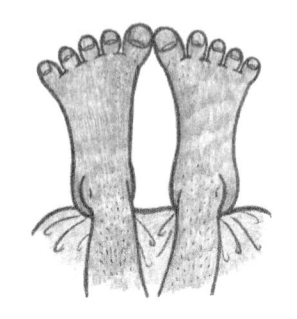

I thought he was supposed to be working but he had his feet up watching the telly.

- ***chanter à tue-tête*** – to sing at the top of one's voice

Literally: to sing at kill-head

Capucine, qui avait un peu trop bu, chantait à tue-tête : « On a besoin de toi, amour ! »

Capucine, who had drunk a bit too much, was singing at the top of her voice, 'We need you, love!'

The adverb *à tue-tête* dates from the 16th century. At that time the verb *tuer* not only meant 'to kill' but had other parallel meanings. It also meant 'to lose consciousness' and 'to tire oneself out' or 'to destroy one's health'. Therefore, *chanter à tue-tête* did not mean 'to sing until dead' but rather 'to sing until tired out'.

- **chanter en yaourt*** – to sing in mangled English

Literally: to sing in yoghurt

Ma sœur n'a jamais été très calée en anglais, et ses enfants se moquent d'elle quand elle chante en yaourt le tube d'Adèle : « Éllo ! Is mi. Ou-o if yé yé-é-é you like to mi ? »

My sister was never brilliant at English, and her children make fun of her when she mangles Adèle's hit song: 'Hello! It's me! I was wondering if after all these years you'd like to meet'.

To be able to sing *en yaourt*, it is essential that the singer knows at least some English, as the overall effect should sound enough like English to be convincing but be incomprehensible to a native English speaker.

- **chanter comme une casserole*** – to be a lousy* singer

Literally: to sing like a saucepan

J'aimerais bien me joindre au Chœur de Rockers mais je chante comme une casserole !

I'd love to join the Rockers' Choir but I'm a lousy singer!

- **Cool, Raoul !* Relax, Max !*** – Chill out !*

    Literally: Cool, Raoul! Relax, Max!

    « *Mon examen est dans deux jours ! Je stresse grave ! Plus rien ne rentre !*

    – *Cool, Raoul ! Relax, Max !* »

'My exam's in two days! I'm seriously stressed out! Nothing's going in anymore!'
'Chill out!'

Cool and *relax* have both been borrowed from the English. 'Raoul' or 'Max' has been added simply for fun and to reinforce the meaning by adding a rhyming word. Other expressions which are similarly playful using rhyme or assonance are:

À l'aise, Blaise ! – at ease!

Tu parles, Charles ! – you bet!

Je te le donne en mille, Émile ! – you'll never guess!

Tu l'as dit, bouffi ! – you said it! (this can come across as rather insulting, so use with care!)
    And see chapter 2 for:

À la tienne Étienne ! – cheers!

- ***croquer la vie à pleines dents*** – to make the most of life

Literally: to bite the life with full teeth

Jamila croque la vie à pleines dents. La semaine dernière elle a fait un saut à l'élastique et la semaine prochaine elle commencera son tour d'Afrique.

Jamila makes the most of life. Last week she did a bungee jump and next week she'll be starting her tour of Africa.

- ***démarrer sur les chapeaux de roues*** – to get off to a fast start *or* a flying start

Literally: to start on the hats of wheels *or* the hubcaps

Avec notre offre spéciale à 11 € les deux parties de bowling et deux boissons par personne, les grandes vacances démarrent sur les chapeaux de roues !

With our special offer of 11€ for two rounds of ten-pin bowling and two drinks per person, the summer holidays get off to a flying start!

The modern French word for a hubcap is *un enjoliveur* but in the early days of motoring, hubcaps were known as *les chapeaux de roues*. Imagine one of those first racing cars turning a corner so fast that the car rocked onto its side and scraped the hubcap on the ground as it went. By extension, this expression was applied to any car travelling fast, then to any activity getting off to a quick start.

- ***être à la fête*** – to be having a field day; to be one's day

Literally: to be at the party

Mathéo, entouré de belles femmes, était à la fête.

Mathéo, surrounded by beautiful women, was having a field day.

- ***être tout feu tout flamme*** – to be wildly enthusiastic; to be full of enthusiasm

Literally: to be all fire all flame

J'ai adoré chanter dans notre concert hier soir ! Ce matin je suis tout feu tout flamme et je me suis déjà mise à apprendre la musique pour notre prochain concert - le Requiem de Mozart !

I loved singing in our concert last night! This morning I'm full of enthusiasm and I've already started learning the music for our next concert – Mozart's Requiem!

- ***faire la fête à quelqu'un*** – to give somebody a warm welcome *or* reception

Literally: to do the party to somebody

Quand je rentre le soir, mon chien, Crockdur, me fait la fête.
When I come home in the evening, my dog, Crockdur, greets me with affection.

Attention ! Not to be confused with **faire sa fête à quelqu'un**** meaning 'to beat somebody up' – *Si tu continues, je vais te faire ta fête*: if you carry on, you're gonna get a good hiding*.

- **faire le lézard* ; lézarder* au soleil** – to bask in the sun

Literally: to make the lizard; to lizard in the sun

Quand on habite dans le Midi, on n'a pas besoin d'aller loin pour faire le lézard. J'aime prendre un bain de soleil dans mon jardin.

When you live in the South of France, you don't need to go far to bask in the sun. I like sunbathing in my garden.

- **faire les quatre cents coups** – to paint the town red; to raise merry hell

Literally: to do the four hundred blows

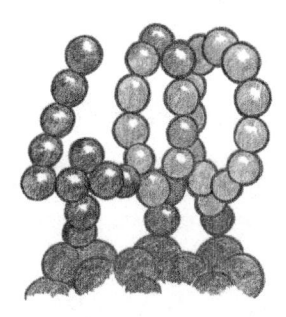

Je ne veux pas passer mes vacances dans un endroit où les jeunes font les quatre cents coups chaque nuit.

I don't want to spend my holidays somewhere where youths raise merry hell every night.

Louis XIII, during his war against Protestantism in 1621, attacked the town of Montauban with four hundred cannonballs. The town still did not surrender, and the four hundred blows went down in history.

François Truffaut, the French film director, made a film in 1959 called *'Les Quatre Cents Coups'*, one of the defining films of the French New Wave. It is about an ordinary adolescent who was considered a troublemaker. The title was translated into English as 'The 400 Blows', which totally misses the real meaning of the French expression ('to raise merry hell' or 'to paint the town red') and led many people to think the title referred to corporal punishment.

- ***faire un tabac*** * – to be a hit

Literally: to make a tobacco

L'album 'Jamais seul' du rocker Johnny Hallyday fit un tabac en France, mais pas en Angleterre.

The album 'Never Alone' by the rock singer Johnny Hallyday was a hit in France, but not in England.

Forget about tobacco! This expression is related to *passer quelqu'un à tabac* and *tabasser quelqu'un*, both meaning 'to beat somebody up'. Though the origin is not clear, it seems that old words coming from French dialects meaning 'to hit' or 'to make a noise or tumult' crossed with the word for tobacco which sounded the same. If an audience is applauding enthusiastically, people are clapping their hands together, and are probably stamping their feet too, making quite a noise or tumult.

- ***marcher (comme) sur des roulettes*** * – to go like clockwork; to go (off) very smoothly

Literally: to work (as) on roller-skates

Tout marchait comme sur des roulettes au Festival Rock en Seine : l'organisation était parfaite, la musique était géniale, le soleil brillait, et tout le monde était bien content.

Everything was going off very smoothly at the Rock Festival on the Seine: the organization was perfect, the music was great, the sun was shining, and everyone was very happy.

- ***Minute papillon !*** – Just a minute! *or* Hold your horses! *or* Not so fast!

Literally: Minute butterfly!

« *Mamie, tu viens avec nous ou pas ?*

- *Minute papillon, j'arrive ! Je cherche mes bottes en caoutchouc.* »

'Granny, are you coming with us or not?'
'Hold your horses! I'm coming! I'm looking for my wellies.'

We know that this expression was first noted in the early 20th century but its origin is disputed. It might simply be that a butterfly flutters around, never staying for long in any one place (the verb *papillonner* is 'to flit around' or 'to switch back and forth from one activity to another'). On the other hand, there might be some truth in a nice little story which could explain the origin of the expression. It is said that, before the Second World War, journalists from the weekly satirical newspaper *Le Canard enchaîné* would frequent a nearby café in Paris where one of the waiters was called Papillon. At times, Papillon struggled to serve his many impatient customers quickly enough, so he would shout, '*Minute, j'arrive !*' To let the flustered waiter know that it was all right to take his time, the journalists would reply, '*Minute Papillon !*' and the expression is said to have been popularised from there.

- **Quand on parle du loup (on en voit la queue) (proverbe)** – Speak of the devil (and he's sure to appear) (proverb)

Literally: When one speaks of the wolf (one sees his tail)

Marie m'a dit que Francis… tiens, Francis ! Quand on parle du loup !

Marie told me that Francis… hey, Francis! Speak of the devil!

Early 17th century dictionaries list this French proverb.

- **s'en donner à cœur joie** – to have a tremendous time; to go to town

Literally: to give oneself of it at heart joy

« *Amusez-vous bien en Australie ! Je suis sûr que vous allez vous en donner à cœur joie !* »

'Enjoy yourselves in Australia! I'm sure you're going to have a tremendous time!'

- ***trouver son bonheur*** – to find what one is looking for *or* what one wants

Literally: to find one's happiness

Finalement, après deux heures en ville, Éric Morin avait trouvé son bonheur : un stylo espion caméra.

Finally, after two hours in town, Éric Morin had found what he was looking for: a spy camera pen.

- ***voir la vie en rose*** – to see everything through rose-coloured spectacles

Literally: to see (the) life in pink

Il est toujours positif et optimiste. Il voit la vie en rose.

He's always positive and optimistic. He sees everything through rose-coloured spectacles.

(i) One of the most famous songs in the French language is that of Édith Piaf, *LaVie en rose*, released as a single in 1947. She wrote the lyrics, and the music was by Louiguy. It became Piaf's signature song and made her internationally famous. It was a hit in the UK and the US in French, and was also translated many times into other languages:

Quand il me prend dans ses bras / Il me parle tout bas / Je vois la vie en rose.

When he takes me in his arms / He speaks to me softly / I see life in rosy hues.

Quiz 3

1. *Les enfants faisaient beaucoup de bruit. Ils chantaient …*
a) *à tue-tête.*
b) *à tuer la tête.*
c) *à la tête.*

2. *Je ne vais pas travailler dans une usine toute ma vie. Je vais croquer la vie …*
a) *à pleines dents.*
b) *à pleine gorge.*
c) *à pleine bouche.*

3. *Arrête, s'il te plaît ! Tu chantes comme …*
a) *une poêle à frire !*
b) *un wok !*
c) *une casserole !*

4. *Quand je rentre, mon chien me fait … Il me lèche et il me saute dessus.*
a) *une fête.*
b) *les fêtes.*
c) *la fête.*

5. *Maria s'amuse comme une folle. Elle est …*
a) *au fait.*
b) *à la fête.*
c) *au faîte.*

6. *Tous les films de Harry Potter ...*
a) *ont fait un tabac.*
b) *ont fait le tabac.*
c) *ont fumé.*

7. *Je ne peux pas sentir Arthur. Je le trouve – tiens, Arthur ! Quand on parle du ... , on en voit la queue !*
a) *loup*
b) *renard*
c) *diable*

8. *Patrick et Blandine ont autorisé Matthias à organiser chez eux une fête pour ses 18 ans. Il est tout feu ... !*
a) *toute femme*
b) *tout flamme*
c) *toute flamme*

9. *Nous allons nous rendre au festival de Rock ce weekend et nous allons nous en donner ...*
a) *à cœur joie.*
b) *à cœur joli.*
c) *à joli cœur.*

10. *Le centre-ville est un peu trop animé pour moi. Les ados font les ... cents coups dans la ville le samedi soir.*
a) *quatre*
b) *quatorze*
c) *quarante*

11. *J'aime les buffets dînatoires parce qu'on peut manger à ...-larigot.*

a) *pousse*
b) *tient*
c) *tire*

12. Serge était très nerveux et stressé la veille de son examen. Il se rongeait les ongles. Pour essayer de le calmer un peu, son ami lui a dit : ...
a) « *Cool, Poule ! Relax, Axe !* »
b) « *Cool, Raoul ! Relax, Max !* »
c) « *Cool, Colin ! Relax, Renaud !* »

13. « Si tu te sens malade, Papi, ne te donne pas la peine de nous accompagner à la fête foraine.
– Minute ... ! J'étais juste un peu fatigué. Ça va maintenant. J'arrive ! »
a) *coccinelle*
b) *libellule*
c) *papillon*

14. Julie cherchait un pull rayé bleu et blanc, et après une heure elle a trouvé ...
a) *le bonheur.*
b) *son bonheur.*
c) *sa bonne heure.*

15. C'était très bien organisé, et tout marchait comme sur des ...
a) *rouleaux.*
b) *roulottes.*
c) *roulettes.*

16. *Louna ne voit jamais le mal dans le monde. Elle voit la vie en …*
a) *vert.*
b) *violet.*
c) *rose.*

17. *Quand il fait du soleil, je fais attention à ma peau et je ne fais jamais …*
a) *le lézard.*
b) *la lézarde.*
c) *le léopard.*

18. *La fête a démarré sur les … de roues.*
a) *bobs*
b) *bonnets*
c) *chapeaux*

19. *Après ses vacances passées en Angleterre, on a souvent entendu Zoé chanter en … sa chanson d'amour préférée : « Only youuu ! »*
a) *crème*
b) *clafoutis*
c) *yaourt*

20. *Lola n'est pas occupée. Elle est en train de se reposer, les doigts de pieds en …*
a) *éventaire.*
b) *éventail.*
c) *éventé.*

Answers 3

1.	a	11.	c
2.	a	12.	b
3.	c	13.	c
4.	c	14.	b
5.	b	15.	c
6.	a	16.	c
7.	a	17.	a
8.	b	18.	c
9.	a	19.	c
10.	a	20.	b

CHAPTER 4

Les rires – laughter

Is there a difference between the French sense of humour and the British sense of humour? Definitely! The British love to make fun of themselves, whereas the French are more likely to take pleasure in mocking others. The premise of the film *Le Dîner de cons*, for example, is that it is a funny idea to invite an idiot to a dinner party so that the other guests can ridicule him.

The French enjoy satire much more than the British. They have two very important satirical magazines, *Charlie Hebdo* (whose offices were attacked in 2015 by gunmen who killed 12 people and injured 11 others) and also *Le Canard enchaîné* which was founded in 1915 and is still widely read. The satirical television show *Les Guignols* (the equivalent of *Spitting Image*) was immensely popular until it came to an end in 2018. It is said to have influenced the outcome of elections.

Word play is very important in comic strips (*Astérix le Gaulois*, for example) and in newspaper headlines. However, according to an article in The Local, Stephen Clarke, the author of several wonderful, funny books on French culture, believes it is not much used in stand-up comedy (*le stand-up*) or on television. In his opinion, French humour is often about shouting and being vulgar. French stand-up comics are also more likely to make jokes about sex, which often don't go down too well with British audiences who find them too shocking.

It was only in 1932 that the Académie française accepted the word *humour* into the French language, borrowed back from the English. This shows what a foreign concept it was! Until then, French humour was talked of in terms of *esprit* (wit), *blagues* (jokes), *farces* (practical jokes) and *bouffonneries* (buffoonery).

- ***c'était à mourir de rire*** – it would make you die laughing; it was hysterical*

Literally: it was to die of laughing

Samedi soir on a téléchargé le film Le Père Noël est une ordure. *Il faut le voir ! C'était à mourir de rire !*

On Saturday night we downloaded the film *Father Christmas is a scumbag*. You must see it! You'd die laughing!

- ***c'était à se rouler par terre**** – it would make you die laughing; it was hysterical*; rolling on the ground *or* floor laughing*

Literally: it was to roll oneself on ground

« *T'as vu ce film sur la natation synchronisée masculine ? Comment s'appelle-t-il déjà ?*

– *Tu veux dire* Le Grand Bain *avec Mathieu Almaric ? Ouais ! C'était à se rouler par terre !* »

'Have you seen that film about male synchronised swimming? What's it called, again?'
'You mean *The Deep End* with Mathieu Almaric? Yeah! It was hilarious!'

According to Rey, this expression was first noted in 1869 and refers to an uncontrollable fit of giggles. Others have suggested that it might come from equestrian circles. Horses like to writhe around on the ground (probably to dislodge pests) and this seems to give them much pleasure.

With a similar meaning, we also have the more vulgar version of this expression: ***à se taper le cul par terre*****

Literally: to bang one's bum* *or* arse*** on the ground

- ***être plié(e) (en deux* ou *en quatre); être plié(e) de rire*** – to be doubled up with laughter

Literally: to be folded (in two *or* in four); to be folded of laughter

J'adore le stand-up de Gad Elmaleh. À chaque fois que je regarde son spectacle L'autre c'est moi, *je suis pliée en deux !*

I love Gad Elmaleh's stand-up comedy. Every time I watch his show The Other One's Me, I'm doubled up with laughter!

ⓘ Gad Elmaleh's description of his English lessons at school, where he learned how to ask that essential question 'Where is Brian?' is not to be missed! *Tu seras plié(e) de rire !*

- ***plus on est de fous, plus on rit !*** – the more the merrier!

Literally: more there is of fools, more one laughs

« *Je peux me joindre à vous ?*
  – *Oui, bien sûr, plus on est de fous, plus on rit !*

'Can I join you?'
'Yes, of course, the more the merrier!'

- ***rira bien qui rira le dernier (proverbe)*** – he who laughs last laughs longest (proverb)

Literally: will laugh well who will laugh the last

La partie n'est pas terminée, Bernard ! Je vais prendre ma revanche. Rira bien qui rira le dernier !
The game's not over, Bernard! I'm going to get my revenge. He who laughs last laughs longest!

- ***rire à gorge déployée*** – to scream *or* roar with laughter

Literally: to laugh with throat opened out *or* spread out *or* unfurled

Regarde ce sketch de Florence Foresti incarnant Isabelle Adjani dans On n'est pas couché *! C'est tordant ! J'ai ri à gorge déployée quand je l'ai vu.*

Watch this sketch of Florence Foresti imitating Isabelle Adjani in *We Haven't Gone to Bed*! It's a scream! I roared laughing when I saw it.

(i) Take this opportunity to google Florence Foresti if you don't know her yet! *Tu riras à gorge déployée !*

- ***rire jaune*** – to give a forced laugh

Literally: to laugh yellow

Monsieur Bonnet, le chef d'établissement, n'aimait pas trop les poissons d'avril et il a ri jaune quand il a remarqué le poisson collé dans le dos de son costume neuf.

Mr Bonnet, the headteacher, didn't much like April Fools' Day pranks and he forced a laugh when he noticed the fish stuck to the back of his new suit.

You might consider yellow to be the colour of all things bright and beautiful, such as sunshine or sparkling gold, but in its duller shades yellow has long been associated with things negative. Two of the more memorable examples of this are the depictions of Judas the traitor, who was dressed in yellow, and the infamous Star of David symbol, which Jews were forced to wear during the Second World War.

Duneton, in his excellent book *La Puce à l'oreille*, cites the use of this expression in 1640, where the writer Oudin notes, '*Il rit jaune comme farine*' (*farine* in the slang of the day did not refer to flour but to someone vicious).

- **se fendre la poire**** ou **la gueule**** ou **la pipe**** ou **la pêche**** – to laugh one's head off *or* to split one's sides laughing

Literally: to split oneself the pear *or* the mouth *or* the pipe *or* the peach

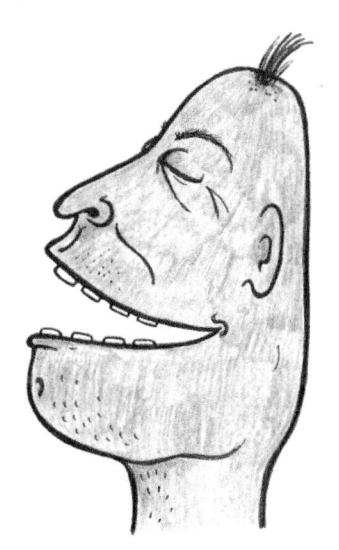

Tu connais le sketch culte de Dany Boon, 'Le K-way' ? Non ? Alors, regarde-le ! Tu te fendras la poire !

Do you know Dany Boon's cult sketch, 'The Cagoule'? No? Well, watch it! You'll split your sides laughing!

La gueule is simply a slang word for the mouth. *La poire* and *la pêche* are slang words for the head or the face as are other round fruits such as *la pomme*. There is a famous caricature of King Louis-Philippe drawn by Charles Philipon in 1832 where the king's head looks like a pear. If the mouth is wide open in laughter, then the face seems split in two.

La pipe is another slang word for the throat (see *casser sa pipe* in chapter 7).

- ***une plaisanterie qui vole bas*** – a feeble joke; a joke in poor taste

Literally: a joke which flies low

Tibor se croit drôle mais ses plaisanteries volent bas.

Tibor thinks he's funny, but his jokes are in poor taste.

Le bonheur – happiness

Much as we love France, it seems that Britain and America are officially happier places than *l'Hexagone*! The UN's World Happiness Report, 2019, listed the UK in 15th place, the US in 19th place, and France in 24th. Finland was the winner for the second year running.

As Tal, the Franco-Israeli singer-songwriter, tells us:

« *Tu sais, rien n'est parfait. / La vie fait des erreurs. / Bats-toi seulement pour le meilleur. / C'est vrai, rien n'est parfait, / Mais chaque seconde de bonheur / Te donne le goût de vivre encore plus fort.* »

'You know nothing is perfect. / Life makes mistakes. / Fight just for the best. / It's true, nothing is perfect, / But every second of happiness / Gives you the taste for living even more strongly.'

('*Rien n'est parfait*' from the 2012 album *Le droit de rêver*.)

- **avoir le moral ; avoir (un) bon moral ; avoir un moral d'acier** – to be in good spirits; to have a high morale

Literally: to have the morale; to have a good morale; to have a morale of steel

A l'approche de la finale, un coureur en grande forme a un moral d'acier.

As the final gets closer, a runner in top form has a high morale.

> Don't confuse *le moral* with *la morale*! *Le moral* in French is 'morale' in English or 'good spirits', whereas *la morale* in French is 'moral doctrine', 'morals' or 'ethics'.

- **être aux anges** – to be in heaven; to be over the moon*

Literally: to be at the angels

Quentin est aux anges d'être enfin papa.

Now that Quentin's a daddy at last, he's over the moon.

- ***je me sentais pousser des ailes*** – I was walking or treading on air; I felt as if I'd grown wings

Literally: I felt myself grow some wings

Le jour où les Bleus ont remporté la Coupe du monde de football, je me suis senti pousser des ailes ! J'ai arrêté de tergiverser : j'ai enfilé mon maillot, et je me suis inscrit dans une équipe de football locale.

The day the Blues won the football World Cup, I felt as if I'd grown wings! I stopped dithering: I put on my strip, and I joined a local football team.

- ***tout baigne (dans l'huile)* ; ça baigne**** – everything's hunky-dory

Literally: everything bathes (in the oil); that bathes

« *Tiens, t'as un nouveau gorille, hein ?*
  – *Mon nouveau garde du corps s'appelle Monsieur Geoffroy, et depuis que je l'ai embauché, tout baigne !* »

'So, you've got a new bodyguard, eh?"
'My new bodyguard is called Mr Geoffroy, and since I've taken him on, everything is hunky-dory!'

This expression started its life as *tout baigne dans l'huile* then other greases were exchanged for oil: *tout baigne dans le beurre* or *dans la margarine.* Now it is mainly heard without reference to any grease, just simply as *tout baigne* or *ça baigne.* The image is to do with mechanical parts which run smoothly if well oiled.

La bonne santé – good health

The French health care system is deemed to be among the best in the world. It is partly funded by compulsory health care insurance and is topped up by the state. You pay a small fee to visit a GP (*un* or *une généraliste*) and once given a prescription, it will cost a little less than in the UK to get your medicines, and a great deal less than in the US (about half the cost). Waiting lists for operations are much shorter than in the UK. In 2016 there were more than twice as many hospital beds in France than in the UK per head of population, and many more doctors and nurses per patient. However, recently, doctors have been complaining loudly that the pressures upon the French health service are becoming too great and that the quality of health care is in decline.

- ***avoir bon pied bon œil*** – to be fit as a fiddle

Literally: to have good foot good eye

« *Comment va ton grand-père, François ?*
  - *Très bien, merci. Il a bon pied bon œil comme toujours.* »

'How's your grandfather, François?'
'Very well, thanks. He's as fit as a fiddle as always.'

He who has a good foot and a good eye is likely to be fit and healthy. This expression goes back to the 17th century and is used mainly in the context of old people.

- ***avoir de l'énergie à revendre*** – to have energy to spare *or* galore *or* in spades*

Literally: to have energy to sell off

J'ai commencé à prendre un café tous les jours vers quinze heures et à faire une petite sieste tout de suite après l'avoir bu. Quand je me réveille vingt minutes plus tard, j'ai de l'énergie à revendre !

I've started taking a coffee every day around 3pm and I take a little nap straight after drinking it. When I wake up twenty minutes later, I've got energy galore!

You can use the phrase '*à revendre*' when you have anything in abundance. For example, you can say, '*Prends des fraises, on en a à revendre !*' – Take some strawberries, we have lots of them!

- ***avoir la frite*** ou ***la patate*** – to feel great; to be in great shape; to have lots of energy

Literally: to have the chip (UK) *or* the French fry (US); to have the potato

Depuis que son fils est retourné au Canada, Franck n'a pas l'air d'avoir la frite.

Since his son returned to Canada, Franck doesn't look too great.

ⓘ You can also substitute other verbs for *avoir* to play around with the expression. For example, **donner la frite**:

A ton avis, qu'est-ce qu'on pourrait faire pour donner la frite à Nadia ?

What do you think we could do to cheer Nadia up *or* to perk Nadia up?

Or maybe **garder la frite**:

J'espère qu'Alain va garder la frite quand il entendra que le sous-chef a rendu son tablier.

I hope Alain is still going to be feeling good when he hears the sous-chef has left.

When the word *patate* first came into the language in the 16th century, it referred to what is now known as *la patate douce* – the sweet potato, but it is currently used quite widely in familiar terms to mean the same as *une pomme de terre* – a potato. Because of its shape and texture, *la patate* was often used in figurative expressions and was sometimes used to mean 'the head'. It is probable that there was an earlier version which would have made a little more sense: *il a une sacrée patate* (if you have a good head, you feel great) then this became more simply *il a la patate.* In the 1970s the variation *avoir la frite* became popular, as chips (UK) or French fries (US) are, of course, made from potatoes.

- **avoir la pêche*** – to be on form; to be in high spirits; to have lots of energy; to be feeling peachy*

Literally: to have the peach

J'ai la pêche aujourd'hui. Ce matin je vais aller à la piscine puis cet après-midi je vais m'attaquer au grand nettoyage de printemps.

I'm on form today. This morning I'm going to go to the swimming pool then this afternoon I'm going to tackle the spring cleaning.

ⓘ You can replace a peach with a banana in this expression: *j'ai la banane !* You can also exaggerate how great you are feeling by saying you have a peach (or a banana) from hell: *'J'ai une pêche d'enfer !'*

- **péter le feu**** – to be full of energy; to be full of beans (UK)

Literally: to fart** the fire

Depuis que Guillaume sort avec sa nouvelle copine, il pète le feu.
Since Guillaume's been going out with his new girlfriend, he's been full of beans.

The verb *péter* can be used to mean 'to explode' *or* 'to burst'. This is a 20th century expression.

- ***reprendre du poil de la bête*** * – to regain strength; to pick up again

Literally: to take back some hair of the beast

« *Tu as été malade, André ?*
  - Oui j'ai été très malade, mais je commence à reprendre du poil de la bête maintenant. »

'Have you been ill, André?'
'Yes, I've been very ill, but I'm starting to pick up again now.'

It is not certain where this expression came from, but it seems that the most likely origin was in the ancient belief that if a dog bit you, applying the skin of the said dog to the wound would help it to heal.

- **se remettre sur pied** – to get back on one's feet

Literally: to put oneself back on foot

Après huit semaines de désintoxication, Bastien se remet doucement sur pied.

After eight weeks of rehab, Bastien is starting to get back on his feet.

Quiz 4

1. *Rira bien qui rira le …*
a) *derrière.*
b) *dernier.*
c) *premier.*

2. *Quand notre prof de maths, Madame Perrin, a vu sa caricature sur le tableau, elle a ri …*
a) *jaune.*
b) *blanc.*
c) *vert.*

3. *Il a raconté une blague raciste, mais c'était une plaisanterie qui volait …*
a) *haut.*
b) *pas.*
c) *bas.*

4. *C'était marrant ! Je me suis fendu …*
a) *le tuyau.*
b) *la pipe.*
c) *la gorge.*

5. *Le jour de notre mariage, je me sentais pousser des …*
a) *ailerons.*
b) *ailes.*
c) *ailiers.*

6. *Fahima fait du vélo, du karaté et de la musculation, et elle nage trois fois par semaine. Elle … le feu !*
a) *pète*
b) *prête*
c) *peste*

7. *Depuis que j'ai commencé à aller à une classe de Zumba Fitness trois fois par semaine, j'ai de l'énergie à … !*
a) *revenir*
b) *revendre*
c) *revendiquer*

8. *Je fais du jogging tous les matins ! J'ai … !*
a) *la pomme de terre*
b) *la frite*
c) *les frites*

9. *Après une longue maladie, elle commence à se remettre…*
a) *sur tête.*
b) *sur bras.*
c) *sur pied.*

10. *Hier j'ai regardé le vieux film* Les Bronzés. *C'était à … de rire.*
a) *tuer*
b) *étrangler*
c) *mourir*

11. *C'est très drôle. J'ai ri à gorge …*
a) *déployée.*
b) *déplorée.*
c) *déplacée.*

12. *« Ça va ?*
– Oui, ça va bien. … »
a) *Tout baigne.*
b) *Tout le monde se baigne.*
c) *Tout se baigne.*

13. *Rafiq a été malade mais il commence à reprendre du poil …*
a) *du bœuf.*
b) *de la bourrique.*
c) *de la bête.*

14. *Je me sens bien aujourd'hui. J'ai …*
a) *l'ananas.*
b) *l'abricot.*
c) *la pêche.*

15. *J'ai passé une excellente journée ! J'ai …*
a) *la morale.*
b) *le moral.*
c) *la moralité.*

16. *T'as vu ce film de Dany Boon, La Ch'tite Famille ? C'est à … !*
a) *rouler sur le parterre*
b) *se rouler sur la partenaire*
c) *se rouler par terre*

17. « Comment va ta grand-mère ?
   – … »
a) *Elle a bonne jambe bon nez.*
b) *Elle a bon pied bon œil.*
c) *Elle a de beaux yeux.*

18. *J'ai vu un film comique qui s'appelle* Oscar *hier soir. J'étais plié en …*
a) *deux.*
b) *trois.*
c) *huit.*

19. *Isaac a demandé Colette en mariage. Elle est aux…*
a) *diables.*
b) *saints.*
c) *anges.*

20. *Viens avec nous ! Plus il y a de fous, … !*
a) *plus on rit*
b) *plus il y a de riz*
c) *il n'y a plus de riz*

Answers 4

1. b
2. a
3. c
4. b
5. b
6. a
7. b
8. b
9. c
10. c
11. a
12. a
13. c
14. c
15. b
16. c
17. b
18. a
19. c
20. a

CHAPTER 5

La négativité – negativity

    To start this chapter on things which are not quite right with the world, how about a little poetry? If you enjoy French poetry, why not explore the website www.poetica.fr which groups poems by theme and by poet. Here then is Paul Verlaine's poem *'Il pleure dans mon cœur'* from his collection of 1874, *Romances sans paroles*.

Il pleure dans mon cœur
Comme il pleut sur la ville ;
Quelle est cette langueur
Qui pénètre mon cœur ?

Ô bruit doux de la pluie
Par terre et sur les toits !
Pour un cœur qui s'ennuie,
Ô le chant de la pluie !

Il pleure sans raison
Dans ce cœur qui s'écœure.
Quoi ! nulle trahison ?...
Ce deuil est sans raison.

C'est bien la pire peine
De ne savoir pourquoi
Sans amour et sans haine
Mon cœur a tant de peine !

And here is my humble attempt at a translation of one of France's greatest and most loved poets!

It is crying in my heart
As it rains on the town;
What is this languor
Which penetrates my heart?

Oh sweet sound of the rain
On the earth and on the roofs!
For a heart which is weary,
Oh the song of the rain!

It cries for no reason
In this heart which is sickened.
What! no treachery?...
This mourning is without reason.

It is indeed the worst sorrow
Not to know why
Without love and without hatred
My heart has so much sorrow!

- ***avoir droit à la soupe à la grimace*** – to get a frosty reception; to be in the doghouse

Literally: to qualify for the grimace soup

Grouille-toi ! On est à la bourre et si on arrive en retard pour l'enterrement, on va avoir droit à la soupe à la grimace !

Get a move on! We are late and if we arrive late for the funeral, we're going to get a frosty reception!

- **ça ne casse pas trois pattes à un canard*** – it's nothing to write home about; it's nothing to get excited about

Literally: that does not break three legs to a duck

« Comment trouves-tu la nouvelle boîte de nuit en ville ?
- Oh, elle ne casse pas trois pattes à un canard. »

'How do you find the new night club in town?'
'Oh, it's nothing to write home about.'

- **ça ne mange pas de pain** – it doesn't cost anything; it can't hurt

Literally: it doesn't eat bread

Quand j'ai déménagé, j'ai demandé à mes parents si je pouvais mettre quelques cartons dans leur garage. Un peu d'espace de rangement, ça ne mange pas de pain.

When I moved to a new house, I asked my parents if I could put some boxes in their garage. A bit of storage space doesn't cost them anything.

When this expression first appeared in the 17th century, bread was a staple food which represented a large proportion of the family's budget. You wouldn't have wanted to risk your daily portion of bread by being over-generous. However, if there were no cost, then why not give freely?

- ***en voir des vertes et des pas mûres*** * – to go through a lot; to experience some hard knocks; to go through the mill

Literally: to see some green ones and some not ripe

L'œil au beurre noir et des hématomes sur la mâchoire, il avait l'air d'en avoir vu des vertes et des pas mûres.

With a black eye and bruises on the jaw, he looked like he'd been through the mill.

Other verbs can be substituted for *voir*. For example:

il en a dit des vertes (et des pas mûres) * – he came out with some pretty risqué stuff*

j'en ai entendu des vertes et des pas mûres sur son compte ! * – you wouldn't believe the things I've heard about him!

The reason the examples above give a range of meanings for this expression is to do with its origin. Expressions combining *le vert* and *le mûr* have been in existence since the 13th century. Depending on the context, *les vertes* might have referred to risqué stories and jokes, or to disagreeable remarks, or anything unpleasant, and all these connotations have been carried through into the modern expression. Fruit which is green is usually not ripe, and for emphasis, the redundant '*les mûres*' has been added. This doubling up is an often-employed rhetorical device.

- ***Est-ce que je te demande si ta grand-mère fait du vélo ?*** – Who asked you for your opinion?; Who asked you to put in your two pennies' worth?* (UK)

Literally: Do I ask you if your grandmother cycles?

« *Tu as intérêt à dire à ton fils de venir te voir plus souvent !*

- *Est-ce que je te demande si ta grand-mère fait du vélo ?* »

'You'd better tell your son to come and see you more often!' 'Who asked you to put in your two pennies' worth?'

This comes from a little ditty from the 1930s. In the song, there are other questions such as, '*si ta p'tite sœur est grande*' – if your little sister is tall, or '*si ton p'tit frère va bien au pot*' – if your little brother is potty-trained.

Now that it is not unusual to see a granny on a bike, some people like to substitute other more modern activities such as *le roller*, *le skate* or *le surf*.

Another expression which has been around since at least the late 19th century and which was often used in a similar situation is:

Et ta sœur ? – Who asked you for your opinion?; Who asked you to put in your two pennies' worth?* (UK)

Literally: And your sister?

ⓘ In times gone by, this might have merited the playful response: '*Ma soeur, elle bat le beurre !*' – my sister is beating the butter!

- **être** ou **rester le bec dans l'eau*** – to be left in the lurch *or* to be left high and dry *or* to be let down

Literally: to be *or* to stay the beak in the water

Mon patron m'a fait de belles promesses d'avancement, mais c'est Delphine qui a été promue, et moi, je suis resté le bec dans l'eau.

My boss made me fine promises of promotion, but it was Delphine who was promoted, and I was left high and dry.

Georges Planelles suggests that, though the link has not been entirely established, the water here might have something to do with the expression *mettre l'eau à la bouche* – to make the mouth water, as we might salivate with the prospect of wonderful things to come, only to be disappointed and to be left with nothing but water in the mouth.

ⓘ There are other figurative expressions which feature *le bec*, such as:

clouer le bec à quelqu'un* – to reduce somebody to silence; to shut somebody up
Literally: to nail somebody's beak

défendre quelque chose bec et ongles – to fight tooth and nail for something
Literally: to defend something beak and (finger)nails

- ***faire tourner quelqu'un en bourrique*** * – to drive somebody to distraction; to drive somebody up the wall

Literally: to make somebody turn into donkey

Il me fait tourner en bourrique à force d'exigences, de taquineries et d'ordres contradictoires.

He's driving me to distraction with his demands, his teasing, and his contradictory orders.

- ***(il ne) faut pas pousser le bouchon trop loin*** – that's pushing it too far

Literally: you must not push the stopper *or* cork *or* cap too far

Si tu veux prendre une bouteille de vin à ton Papa, prends un vin de table et pas son Pouilly Fuissé. Il ne faut pas pousser le bouchon trop loin !

If you want to take a bottle of wine from your dad, take a bottle of table wine and not his Pouilly Fuissé. That's going too far!

ⓘ In 2001 Nestlé launched a series of hugely popular adverts for its chocolate mousses, ChocoSui's, which featured a little boy called Lucas. In the most successful of these adverts, Lucas hears his mother coming into the kitchen where he is just polishing off his third chocolate mousse. The little boy throws his spoon into the goldfish bowl and tells his mother that Maurice, his fish, has eaten them all. With chocolate smeared all over his cute face, he leans over the goldfish bowl and scolds his fish, saying: '*Tu pousses le bouchon un peu trop loin, Maurice!*' The advert won the '*coup de cœur du public*' award at the *Festival Pub et Humour de Paris*. A quick internet search will still find it!

- ***il ne faut pas pousser mémé** ou **mémère** ou **grand-mère dans les orties*** ou **dans les bégonias**** – that's pushing it too far; let's not get carried away; you must not be antisocial

Literally: you must not push granny *or* grandma *or* grandmother in the nettles *or* in the begonias

On a déjà demandé à Anne-Marie de travailler deux dimanches de suite. Alors, un troisième ? Non, il ne faut pas pousser mémé dans les orties !

Anne-Marie has already been asked to work two Sundays in a row. So, a third? No, that's pushing it too far!

The verb *pousser* took on the colloquial meaning of 'to exaggerate' in the 1960s. The 'granny in the nettles' part was later added for fun and to reinforce the meaning. Poor granny!

(i) The popular author Aurélie Valognes wrote a best-selling, feel-good novel in 2015 called *Mémé dans les orties*, in which a grumpy old man does his best to annoy his bullying *concierge*. When his dog goes missing, his mood plummets, but a precocious young girl and a perky elderly neighbour come and brighten up his life.

Each chapter of the book has a French expression or proverb as its title – highly recommended for a fun read!

(i) There is an excellent, funny song by the singer-songwriter Juliette called *Mémère dans les orties*. It is an affectionate duet between two lovers exchanging insults. They only stop arguing as they risk being late for their wedding!

- ***(il ne) manquait plus que ça !*** – that's the last thing I (*or* you, etc.) needed!; that's all I (*or* you, etc.) needed!

Literally: nothing more was missing except that

Je venais de faire réparer le pneu crevé et je me suis remis en route à tombeau ouvert, mais deux minutes plus tard, j'ai entendu les sirènes de police derrière moi. Manquait plus que ça !

I had just had the puncture repaired and I took to the road again at breakneck speed, but two minutes later, I heard the police sirens behind me. That's the last thing I needed!

- ***il y a anguille sous roche*** – something is hidden; something is afoot; something fishy is going on

Literally: there is eel under rock

Quand on lui a demandé de verser 3 000 € sur un compte bancaire à l'étranger, Pierre a commencé à se douter qu'il y avait anguille sous roche.

When he was asked to pay 3,000 € into an overseas bank account, Pierre began to suspect that there was something fishy going on.

Rabelais used this expression in 1532 but it is probably even older than that. Eels were very popular as a culinary ingredient in the Middle Ages, but to catch one during the day, a fisherman would have needed to look under rocks where they would be hiding (eels being bottom-feeders are more active at night time). Hence the idea of something being hidden. Also, the eel is snake-like in appearance and serpents have long been associated with low cunning and deceitfulness.

- **il n'y a pas de quoi pavoiser !** – it's nothing to get excited about *or* to write home about!

Literally: there is nothing about which to deck with flags

« Que pensez-vous des projets pour améliorer la vie culturelle de la ville ?
- *Eh bien, il n'y a pas de quoi pavoiser et il n'y a rien de vraiment nouveau. »*

'What do you think of the plans to improve the cultural life of the town?'

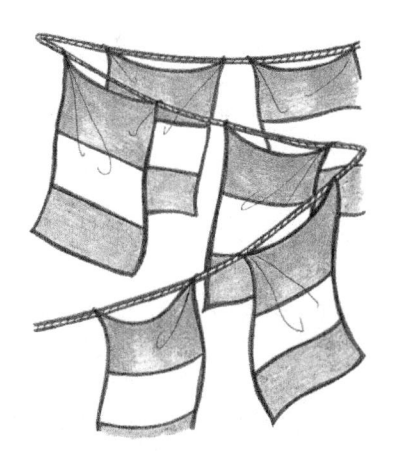

'Well in short, they're nothing to get excited about and there's nothing really new.'

- ***jamais deux sans trois*** – good *or* bad things come in threes; three is the magic number

Literally: never two without three

> *Jamais deux sans trois : après avoir gagné le tournoi deux années de suite, Roger va-t-il être victorieux une troisième fois ?*

> All good things come in threes: after having won the tournament two years in a row, is Roger going to be victorious a third time?

- ***je n'y suis pour rien*** – I have nothing to do with it; it's nothing to do with me

Literally: I am not there for anything

> *C'est mon mari qui a oublié de fermer la porte à clé. On nous a cambriolés mais je n'y suis pour rien.*

> It's my husband who forgot to lock the door. We were burgled but it's nothing to do with me.

ⓘ There is a very moving song called '*Je n'y suis pour rien*' written and performed by the Muslim singer-songwriter Slimane (winner of *The Voice: la plus belle voix* in 2016). He sings beautifully of the distress he feels after the terrorist attack which destroyed the World Trade Centre. You can easily find a video by looking online.

> « *Je vous le jure, je n'y suis pour rien*
> *Et toutes vos injures, me font de la peine, augmente mon chagrin.*
> *Le Dieu que je prie, prône la paix*
> *Valorise la vie, enseigne le respect.* »

'I swear to you, it has nothing to do with me
And all your insults hurt me, increase my sorrow.
The God I pray to advocates peace
Values life, teaches respect.'

- **mon sang n'a fait qu'un tour** – I saw red; it made my blood boil; it made my blood run cold

Literally: my blood made only one turn

Quand je l'ai entendu attaquer ma sœur, mon sang n'a fait qu'un tour, et je l'ai mis KO d'un coup de poing dans le nez.

When I heard him attack my sister, I saw red, and I knocked him down with a punch on the nose.

This is not an expression which makes complete biological sense, perhaps, but it has the meaning of a sudden increase in heart rate accompanied by a strong, angry emotion or an immediate reaction to an event. It comes from an expression dating from around 1790, *tourner les sangs*, which meant 'to be extremely worried'.

- **ne pas en mener large ; n'en mener pas large** – to have one's heart in one's boots; to be feeling worried and lacking in confidence ; to be in a difficult *or* embarrassing situation and to let this show; to feel intimidated

Literally: to not lead large of it

Je n'osais pas croiser le regard du directeur. J'étais sûr qu'il allait me punir. Je n'en menais pas large.

I didn't dare look the head teacher in the eye. I was sure he was going to punish me. My heart was in my boots.

(i) You are only likely to come across this expression in the negative.

- **partir en cacahuète* ou cacahouète*** – to go to the dogs*; to go downhill

Literally: to leave *or* go off in peanut

Hier soir je suis allée au théâtre pour voir une nouvelle pièce. Ça se passait à merveille jusqu'à ce que l'acteur principal oublie ses répliques et là, tout est parti en cacahuète.

I went to the theatre last night to see a new play. It was going beautifully until the leading man forgot his lines, and then it all went downhill.

- **se plaindre pour un pet de travers**** – to be always complaining about one's health

Literally: to complain for a fart askew

Enzo est allé chez le médecin trois fois cette semaine pour un pet de travers !

Enzo has been three times to the doctor's this week for some piffling complaint!

Les maladies et la physiologie – illnesses and physiology

If you cut your hand in two when trying to cut through the stale end of a baguette (*le quignon* or *le croûton*), or you have any medical emergency which requires hospital treatment, you can dial 18 and you will be connected to the *sapeurs-pompiers* (the fire service). They will then redirect you to the SAMU (*le Service d'Aide Médical d'Urgence*) which will send out an ambulance. The number 18 is the general emergency number in France (like 999 in the UK or 911 in the US) so you can use it for police, fire or ambulance. Don't be surprised if *les pompiers* attend your medical emergency because in some parts of the country they have paramedic teams.

You can also use the standard European emergency number which is 112. However, if you call 112 from a mobile phone very close to a border with another country, in Alsace for example, you might be connected to the service of the neighbouring country.

There are several other emergency numbers, but 18 or 112 is all you really need to know.

- ***à vos souhaits !* / à tes souhaits !**** – bless you!

Literally: to your wishes

« *Atchoum ! Atchoum ! Atchoum !*
 – *À vos souhaits !* »

'Atishoo! Atishoo! Atishoo!'
'Bless you!'

ⓘ If you sneeze a second time, you might hear, '**À tes/vos amours !**' – to your loves, and for a third sneeze, '**Et que les tiennes/les vôtres durent toujours !**' – and may yours last forever!

According to polite society, the best thing to do when someone sneezes is to ignore it. After all, a sneeze is an uncontrolled biological reaction and just as one should not comment if someone breaks wind, so too, no comment should be made when someone sneezes. Having said that, many people do still reply to a sneeze with '*À vos souhaits !*'

Newborn babies are prone to sneezing, so what a good idea, in celebration of new life, to pray that their wishes might be fulfilled when they sneeze by saying, '*À tes souhaits !*' But in the Middle Ages when almost half of the population of Europe died of the plague, a sneeze was the first sign of infection and death was likely to follow. You would certainly have wanted to wish someone well if they started to sneeze!

The saying goes back much further than the Middle Ages, however. Théodore de Joliment, an early 19th century writer and historian, believed that the tradition of hoping for somebody that all their wishes might come true when they sneeze goes back to ancient mythology and to early Jewish and Christian teachings, where it is associated not only with the celebration of birth but also with the coming of death. In ancient mythology, Prometheus created an artificial man. The first sign of life this artificial man gave was a sneeze. In the Bible when God blew upon Adam (his first human creation), Adam's first act was to sneeze, and it was also his final act.

- ***avoir la chair de poule*** – to have goose bumps *or* goose pimples

Literally: to have the flesh of chicken

Tu as vu le petit maillot qu'il porte avec ce froid de canard ? J'ai la chair de poule rien qu'en le regardant !

Have you seen the little vest he's wearing in this freezing cold? I've got goose bumps just looking at him!

Quiz 5

1. « À mon avis, ta fille n'aurait pas dû te parler comme ça !
– Est-ce que je te demande si … fait du vélo ? »
a) ton grand-père
b) ta belle-sœur
c) ta grand-mère

2. Mon fils est impossible ! Il me fait tourner en …
a) bourrique.
b) bourgeois.
c) bourdon.

3. Encore un retard ! …
a) Il ne manquait plus que ça !
b) Il ne me manquait pas !
c) Il ne manquait plus rien !

4. Pour les quatre-vingts ans de Sébastien, son frère a voulu l'emmener à un spectacle de strip-tease, mais j'ai dit qu'il ne fallait pas pousser mémé dans …
a) les roses.
b) les chardons.
c) les orties.

5. « Atchoum !
– … »
a) À vos souffrances !
b) À vos sueurs !
c) À vos souhaits !

6. *Vendredi soir, j'ai oublié de dire à ma femme que je dînais avec des collègues. Quand je suis rentré à 22 heures, c'était la soupe … !*
a) *à la limace*
b) *à la grimace*
c) *à la graisse*

7. *Avec les résultats que tu viens d'avoir en maths, tu demandes à sortir ?! Tu pousses … un peu loin !*
a) *ta bouche*
b) *le boucher*
c) *le bouchon*

8. *Tanguy a fait une bêtise : il a mis une invitation à sa fête d'anniversaire sur les réseaux sociaux. Quand trois cents fêtards sont arrivés, tout est complètement parti en …*
a) *cacahuète.*
b) *cacao.*
c) *cacatoès.*

9. *« Tu as entendu son nouveau single ?*
– Oui mais ça ne casse pas trois pattes à … »
a) *un cygne.*
b) *un manchot.*
c) *un canard.*

10. *En salle d'interrogatoire au commissariat de police, le jeune homme n'en menait pas …*
a) *long.*
b) *large.*
c) *gros.*

11. *Il est hypocondriaque ; il se plaint pour ... de travers.*
a) *un pou*
b) *un pet*
c) *un pot*

12. *« Tu aimes leur nouvel album ?*
– Il n'y a pas ... pavoiser. »
a) *quoi*
b) *de*
c) *de quoi*

13. *Ce n'est pas moi qui ai cassé le vase préféré de maman. Je n'y suis ... rien !*
a) *de*
b) *pour*
c) *à*

14. *Je trouve ça très suspect. Je pense qu'il y a ... sous roche.*
a) *serpent*
b) *poisson*
c) *anguille*

15. *Je l'ai salué, mais il ne m'a même pas regardé. Un sourire, ça ne mange pas de ... !*
a) *pin*
b) *pain*
c) *peine*

16. Léa nous a promis des vacances au ski cette année, mais finalement, après toutes ses belles paroles, on est restés … dans l'eau.
a) *la bouche*
b) *le bec*
c) *la tête*

17. Il a passé vingt ans dans la marine. Il en a vu …
a) *des vertes et des pas mûres.*
b) *des pas mûres et des vertes.*
c) *des murs et des fruits verts.*

18. Quand on a annoncé la mauvaise nouvelle du meurtre du policier, mon sang …
a) *n'a pas tourné.*
b) *n'a fait qu'une tour.*
c) *n'a fait qu'un tour.*

19. C'est bien évident qu'il va y avoir un troisième référendum. Jamais … !
a) *deux sans trois*
b) *trois sans quatre*
c) *un plus deux*

20. J'ai froid. Regarde, j'ai…
a) *la chair de poule.*
b) *la poule.*
c) *la chair de pull.*

Answers 5

1.	c	11.	b
2.	a	12.	c
3.	a	13.	b
4.	c	14.	c
5.	c	15.	b
6.	b	16.	b
7.	c	17.	a
8.	a	18.	c
9.	c	19.	a
10.	b	20.	a

CHAPTER 6

Les maladies et la physiologie (suite) – illnesses and physiology (cont.)

According to the European Commission's Eurostat website, a child born in France in 2016 could expect to live 64.1 years of healthy life existence, whereas a child born in the UK could expect to fall into decrepitude a whole year earlier.

- ***avoir les jambes en coton**** ou ***en flanelle**** – to have legs like jelly

Literally: to have the legs in cotton *or* in flannel

Quand je dois passer des examens, j'ai des palpitations et les jambes en coton.

When I have to sit exams, I get palpitations and my legs turn to jelly.

- ***avoir les nerfs à fleur de peau*** – to be over-sensitive *or* irritable; to be all on edge

Literally: to have the nerves on the surface of the skin

Je vous préviens, il a les nerfs à fleur de peau, et on croirait qu'il va fondre en larmes.

I warn you, he's all on edge and he looks likely to burst into tears.

In this expression, the word *fleur* comes from the Latin *florem* (the accusative singular of *flos*). As well as having the literal meaning of 'flower', it also means 'the finest part of something', 'the upper part' or 'the surface'.

Other similar expressions are:
être à bout de nerfs (to be at the end of nerves)

avoir les nerfs à vif (to have frayed/lively nerves)

avoir les nerfs en boule (to have nerves in a ball)

avoir les nerfs en pelote (also to have nerves in a ball)

and ***c'est une vraie boule/pelote de nerfs*** (he/she is a real ball of nerves).

- ***avoir mal au cœur*** – to feel sick

Literally: to have pain in the heart

Ma fille Sarah est venue me dire qu'elle avait mal au cœur, et deux secondes plus tard elle a vomi sur mes chaussures !

My daughter Sarah came to tell me that she felt sick, and two seconds later she vomited on my shoes!

It is strange that the heart could be blamed for an illness which is the stomach's fault! The reason seems to be the meeting of Latin and Greek and a poor understanding of anatomy. The French word for heart, *cœur*, came from the Latin, *cor, cordis*, but the adjective, *cardiaque*, came from the Greek, *kardia.* It was Greek men of learning who mistakenly gave a part of the stomach the name *orifice cardiaque* (the cardiac orifice) and it is because of this that the confusion arose in the 13th century and has remained in the language ever since.

ⓘ **Avoir un haut-le-cœur** (invariable in the plural: *des haut-le-cœur*) is 'to retch' or 'to gag'.

Don't confuse this expression with the rousing call '**Haut les cœurs !**' meaning 'lift up your spirits! take heart! be brave! have courage!'

- **avoir un chat dans la gorge** – to have a frog in the throat

Literally: to have a cat in the throat

« *Je passe la parole à Jean qui va nous présenter les chiffres.*

- *Alors, comme vous le voyez…* (Jean tousse) *… Excusez-moi, j'ai un chat dans la gorge.* »

'I'll hand you over to Jean who is going to present us with the figures.'

'So, as you can see… *(Jean coughs)* … Excuse me, I have a frog in the throat.'

Why a cat in the throat? One possible explanation has been offered by Pierre Guiraud in his *les locutions françaises* (1961). The French word for a tomcat is *un matou* and there may have been a play on words with the similar word *maton*. *Maton* originally meant 'curd' and by extension 'a hair or dust ball' which might catch in the throat (when you are ill and have phlegm in the throat, this is curd-like).

Whether or not this is a likely origin, when you have to clear your throat, it does feel like you are clearing something hairy (or cat-like) from it. It seems a more obvious choice than a frog!

- ***avoir un cheveu sur la langue*** – to lisp

Literally: to speak with a hair on the tongue

À trois ans, un enfant qui a un cheveu sur la langue, c'est mignon, mais à l'âge adulte, ça peut être un vrai handicap.

At three, a child with a lisp is cute, but in adulthood, it can be a real handicap.

ⓘ Someone who speaks with a lisp in French would have difficulty with words containing a *j* or *ch*, so '*j'ai un cheveu sur la langue*' would be pronounced '*z'ai un ceveu sur la langue*'. The verb 'to lisp' in French is *zézayer* or *zozoter*.

The origin is easy to guess: if you have a lisp, you speak as if there is something on your tongue preventing you from articulating clearly, and a hair would do just that.

- ***avoir un coup de barre*** * – to feel drained *or* shattered quite suddenly

Literally: to have a blow of bar

« Allez ! On va en boîte. Tu viens, Arthur ?
  – Non, j'ai un coup de barre. Je rentre. »

'Right, we're going to a nightclub! Are you coming, Arthur?'
'No, I suddenly feel shattered. I'm going home.'

The figurative expression *avoir un coup de barre* has been in the language since the 19th century. Imagine being hit by an iron bar and you would indeed feel shattered!

This expression should not be confused with **c'est le coup de barre* dans ce restaurant**, meaning 'you pay through the nose in this restaurant'.

- **avoir un coup de mou*** – to suddenly feel weak, limp *or* lethargic; to slacken off

Literally: to have a blow of soft *or* slack *or* limp

J'ai enchaîné beaucoup de matchs, et c'est vrai que j'ai eu un petit coup de mou. Ça peut arriver de temps en temps, mais je ne suis pas inquiet.

I've had a lot of matches one after the other, and it's true I slackened off a little for a moment. That can happen from time to time, but I'm not worried.

- ***avoir un coup de pompe*** * – to feel drained *or* shattered quite suddenly

Literally: to have a blow of pump

Oh, j'ai un coup de pompe cet après-midi. Je suis rentrée à trois heures du mat' et maintenant je suis vidée.

Oh, I'm shattered this afternoon. I got in at three in the morning and now I've run out of energy.

Why *un coup de pompe*? Think of a suction pump, *une pompe aspirante.* Now think of a shoe with a hole in it and going for a walk on a wet day. All the water and air is sucked up into the shoe with the foot acting as a pump. That's how the word *pompe* gained the slang meaning of 'shoe' in the 19th century. According to Rey, by extension *pompe* came to mean 'foot' and then 'leg', so *un coup de pompe* is 'a sudden weakness in the legs' and has generalised to meaning 'a feeling of sudden tiredness'.

However, Expressio gives an alternative explanation which comes from the field of aviation. The expression was first noted in 1922 when a pilot, having landed with a planeload of badly shaken passengers, remarked, *'Tu parles qu'on a pris un de ces coups de pompe !'* Aviators used the word *pompe* to describe a rising thermal which carried the plane high (it was as if the air was being pumped up). When the plane leaves a thermal, the air becomes much bumpier, and the plane might rapidly lose height. You often hear people talking of 'hitting an air pocket' when the plane suddenly falls a thousand feet as it leaves a thermal. *Un coup de pompe* is like that terrible sinking feeling or like the feeling you might have after being shaken and buffeted around in an aeroplane.

- **avoir un (petit) grain*** – to have a touch of madness; to be a bit touched

Literally: to have a (little) grain

Il a un petit grain ce garçon ! Il aime jouer au chien et il me lèche le visage !

He's a bit touched that boy! He likes pretending to be a dog and he licks my face!

ⓘ This expression is short for **avoir un petit grain de folie** – to have a little grain of madness.

- **avoir une case (de) vide* ; avoir une case en moins*** – to have a screw loose

Literally: to have a square (of) empty; to have one square less

- **il lui manque une case*** – he's got a screw loose

Literally: he is missing a square

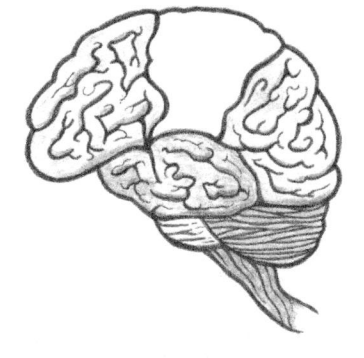

Mon beau-frère, il lui manque une case. Il croit que la fin du monde va arriver dans un an.

My brother in law has got a screw loose. He thinks the world is going to end in a year.

If you think of the brain as being made up of little compartments or *cases,* then someone who is missing a compartment is not normal.

être à l'ouest* – to be out of it* *or* not with it*; to be unable to concentrate; to have one's head in the clouds

Literally: to be at the West

Ça va, Maël ? Tu as l'air à l'ouest ce matin !

Are you OK, Maël? You don't look with it today!

Various theories have been put forward as to the origin of this late 20th century expression, but no-one really knows where it comes from.

- **être dans tous ses états** – to be in a terrible state; to be in a state of extreme agitation

Literally: to be in all one's states

N'étant pas sûre que Christophe fût l'homme de ses rêves, Adiba était dans tous ses états un quart d'heure avant la cérémonie de mariage.

Not being sure that Christophe was the man of her dreams, Adiba was in a terrible state a quarter of an hour before the wedding.

- ***être myope comme une taupe*** – to be as blind as a bat

Literally: to be short-sighted as a mole

Je suis myope comme une taupe sans mes verres de contact.

I'm as blind as a bat without my contact lenses.

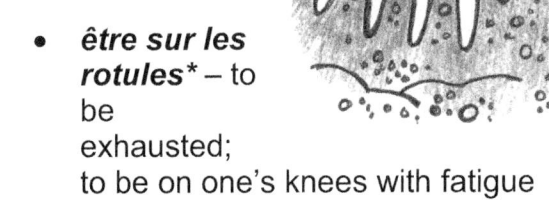

- ***être sur les rotules*** * – to be exhausted; to be on one's knees with fatigue

Literally: to be on the kneecaps

Chéri, tu devrais travailler moins ! Tu vas finir sur les rotules !

Darling, you should work less! You're going to end up exhausted!

ⓘ You can equally use the expression ***être sur les genoux*** – to be on one's knees, which more literally translates the English version.

❗ Be careful not to confuse this with the expression ***être à genoux (devant quelqu'un)*** which means 'to be on one's knees (before someone)' i.e. to kneel in submission.

- **_faire un mal de chien*_** – to really hurt

Literally: to make a hurt of dog

« *Comment va ton dos, Amandine ?*
  – *Ça me fait un mal de chien ! »*

'How's your back, Amandine?'
'It's really hurting!'

Expressions about dogs usually have a connection with extremes. In times past the dog was not seen as man's best friend but rather as a dirty creature not to be trusted.

This expression is not to be confused with **avoir un mal de chien** meaning 'to have great difficulty'. For example, '*J'ai eu un mal de chien à me lever ce matin*' (I had great difficulty getting out of bed this morning).

- **_filer un mauvais coton*_** – (physically) to be very low; to be in a bad way; to be wasting away; (morally) to be getting into bad ways

Literally: to spin a bad cotton

On lui a diagnostiqué un cancer du poumon. Papa file un mauvais coton.

He's been diagnosed with lung cancer. Dad's in a bad way.

This expression, dating from the 19th century, comes from an earlier one, *jeter un vilain coton*, which meant 'to ruin oneself'. It referred to the bobbles you get on an old garment as it starts to wear out.

It is not easy to spin cotton, and if you were to get it all tangled up, you would be in a bad way. There is a related slang expression, **c'est coton**, meaning 'it's difficult'.

- **je ne suis pas dans mon assiette*** – I'm not feeling quite myself; I'm feeling a bit off-colour

Literally: I am not in my plate

Je ne suis pas dans mon assiette aujourd'hui. Je crois que je couve la grippe.

I'm not feeling quite myself today. I think I'm coming down with flu.

The word assiette is linked to the phrase *asseoir quelqu'un*, 'to sit somebody down'. In modern French *une assiette* means not only 'a plate' but also 'a horse rider's seat or stability and posture in the saddle'.

Think back to the time before knives and forks, pre-16th century, when people were seated around the table and ate from a communal plate in the centre of the table. Your *assiette* was your position at the table. If you are not feeling in your *assiette*, then you are not happy with your stability or position; you are feeling ill at ease in a situation or by extension feeling physically ill.

- **je suis à côté de mes pompes*** – I'm not quite with it; I'm really out of it

Literally: I am next to my shoes

- ***marcher à côté de ses pompes**** – to be not quite with it; to have one's head in the clouds

Literally: to walk next to one's shoes

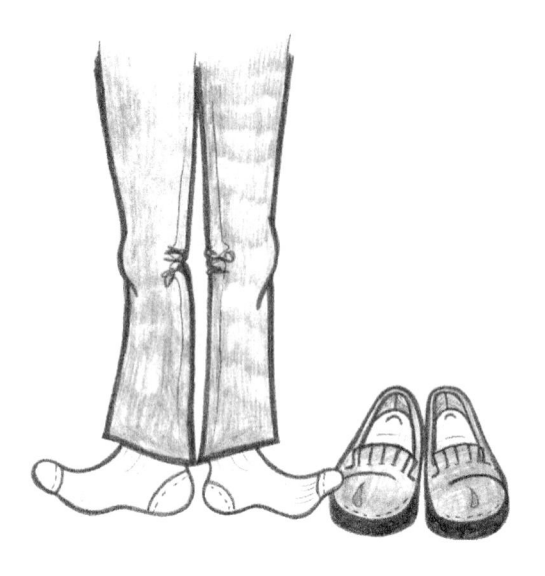

J'ai très mal dormi et je n'arrive pas à me concentrer ; je suis vraiment à côté de mes pompes en ce moment !

I slept really badly and I can't concentrate; I'm really not with it at the moment!

- ***je suis* ou *je me sens mal dans ma peau*** – I'm ill at ease with myself; I don't feel comfortable in my body; things aren't right with me

Literally: I am *or* I feel bad in my skin

De manière générale, depuis notre divorce, mon fils se sent mal dans sa peau.

Generally speaking, since our divorce, my son is ill at ease with himself.

- ***je suis mal dans mes pompes*** * – I'm ill at ease with myself; things aren't right with me

Literally: I am bad in my shoes

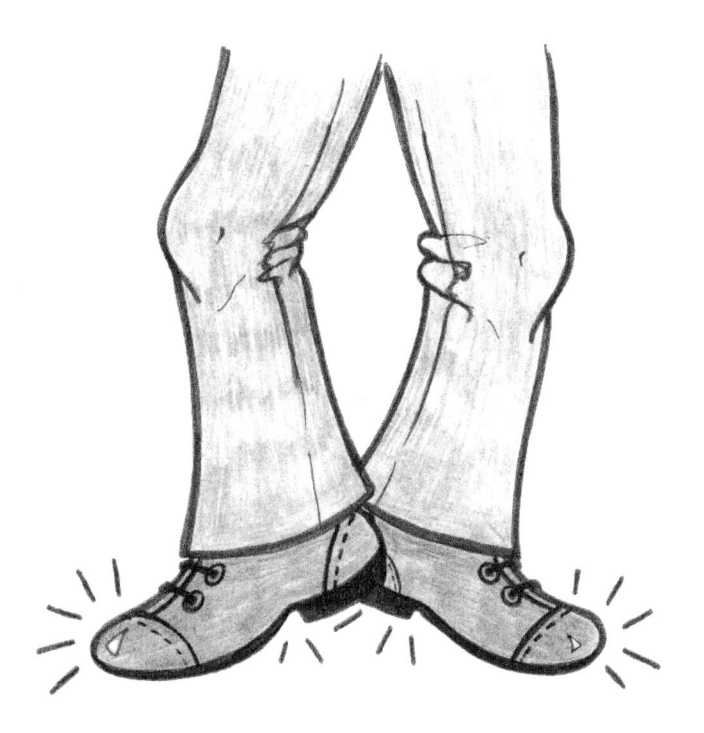

Ma fille a un problème de poids et ça l'empêche de se faire facilement des amis. Elle est mal dans ses pompes, quoi !

My daughter has a weight problem and it prevents her from making friends easily. Things just aren't right with her!

(i) This expression works best in the negative but can be used positively:

être à l'aise ou **bien dans ses pompes** – to feel good

Literally to be at ease *or* well in one's shoes

Quiz 6

1. *Où sont mes lunettes ? Je suis myope comme ... sans elles.*
a) *un tapir*
b) *une taupe*
c) *une taupinière*

2. *« Fabienne est folle !*
– Oui en effet, elle a ... »
a) *une petite graine.*
b) *un petit grain.*
c) *un petit grand.*

3. *Sa santé se dégrade ; il file ...*
a) *une mauvaise laine.*
b) *un mauvais coton.*
c) *une mauvaise soie.*

4. *Je travaille de 7 h à midi et puis j'ai souvent un coup de ... et je dois faire un petit somme.*
a) *pompe*
b) *plomb*
c) *pomme*

5. *« Ça va, Émile ?*
– Non, je ne suis pas dans mon ... aujourd'hui. »
a) *bol*
b) *assiette*
c) *plat*

6. « Tu as la nausée ?
– Oui, j'ai un peu mal … »
a) *au corps.*
b) *par cœur.*
c) *au cœur.*

7. Je peux avoir un petit verre d'eau, s'il vous plaît ?
J'ai … dans la gorge.
a) *une grenouille*
b) *un crapaud*
c) *un chat*

8. Je suis tellement nerveuse ! J'ai les jambes en …
a) *cuir.*
b) *polyester.*
c) *coton.*

9. Je me suis cogné le pied contre la table et ça me fait un mal de …
a) *chien.*
b) *chat.*
c) *chiot.*

10. J'ai besoin d'aide pour retrouver un peu de calme dans ma vie. J'ai les nerfs …
a) *à fleur de peau.*
b) *en fleur.*
c) *à fleur en pot.*

11. J'ai du mal à me concentrer aujourd'hui. Je suis ... mes pompes.
a) à coté de
b) derrière
c) en face de

12. Merci pour vos messages touchants. J'ai eu un petit coup de ..., mais me revoilà en forme !
a) maux
b) molle
c) mou

13. Il faut que je dorme. Je ne veux pas être ... demain !
a) à l'ouest
b) au nord
c) à l'est

14. « Il s'inquiète beaucoup ?
– Oui, il est ... »
a) aux États-Unis.
b) dans tous ses tas.
c) dans tous ses états.

15. Mon fils ne dit pas « joli » ; il dit « zoli ». Il a ... sur la langue.
a) des chevaux
b) un cheval
c) un cheveu

16. *Si tu as un coup de ..., prends un café serré et saute sous la douche.*
a) *bar*
b) *barbe*
c) *barre*

17. *Nicolas a perdu sa joie de vivre et il se déteste. Vraiment il se sent mal dans ...*
a) *sa peau.*
b) *son pot.*
c) *son pull.*

18. *Depuis le jour où ma petite amie m'a plaqué, je suis mal dans mes ...*
a) *pompiers.*
b) *pompes.*
c) *pommes.*

19. *Dieu merci, je suis en vacances dès ce soir ! Je suis sur les ... !*
a) *roulettes*
b) *rotules*
c) *rouleaux*

20. *Si tu penses que je vais voyager jusqu'à l'autre bout du monde pour te voir, c'est qu'il te manque ... !*
a) *un cas*
b) *un carré*
c) *une case*

Answers 6

1. b   11. a
2. b   12. c
3. b   13. a
4. a   14. c
5. b   15. c
6. c   16. c
7. c   17. a
8. c   18. b
9. a   19. b
10. a   20. c

CHAPTER 7

Les maladies et la physiologie (suite) – illnesses and physiology (cont.)

The English are rather squeamish about putting medicines up their bottoms but not so the French! Suppositories (*les suppositoires*) are a great way to get fast-acting pain relief and if you go to a pharmacist to get paracetamol for your baby, it is very likely you will be offered suppositories. You won't find liquid Calpol in France – its equivalent is Doliprane.

- **ne pas avoir les yeux en face des trous*** – to not see clearly what is in front of you; to be not with it*; to be half asleep; to be too tired to think straight

Literally: to not have the eyes facing the holes

« *Attention ! Tu verses du café partout !*
- *Quoi ? Oh, pardon ! Je n'ai pas les yeux en face des trous !* »

'Watch out! You're pouring coffee everywhere!'
'Oh sorry! I'm half asleep!'

ⓘ If you drag yourself out of bed in the morning only half awake, despite having your eyes open, you might well bump into the bedroom door, trip over that toy your toddler left out, and pour orange juice onto your cornflakes. You don't have *les yeux en face des trous!* Or maybe you have been working hard into the small hours trying to get your figures to add up correctly, but you reach the point where nothing makes sense any more. You might well say, '*Je n'ai plus les yeux en face des trous*'. The eyeballs might still be in their sockets, but they appear not to be facing forwards!

You don't have to use this expression in the negative. You can say, for example, '*Il aurait bien besoin d'avoir les yeux en face des trous*' – he really needs to be wide awake and see clearly.

In the 17th century, the expression was *avoir les yeux de travers* – to have the eyes crooked.

- **passer sur le billard*** – to have an operation

Literally: to go onto the snooker table

J'ai reçu deux balles dans le bide dans une embuscade. Je suis passé sur le billard et on m'a recousu.

I got two bullets in the belly in an ambush. I had an operation and they sewed me up again.

The word *billard* first referred only to the curved stick used to play an early form of billiards, which was later replaced by a straight stick. By extension, it became the name of the actual game and the word for the stick changed to *la queue*. By the late 19th century, the word *billard* was also in current use metaphorically to mean 'flat terrain'. Soldiers in the First World War used *le billard* to refer to the flat terrain on the other side of their trenches. Calling an operating table *un billard* because of its flat, rectangular shape, was just another example of this type of metaphor already in use in the early 20th century.

- **perdre les pédales*** – to get all mixed up; to lose one's head *or* marbles*

Literally: to lose the pedals

Ma grand-mère a commencé à perdre les pédales : hier elle a mis son porte-monnaie dans le frigo et le beurre dans son sac à main.

My grandmother is starting to lose her marbles: yesterday she put her purse in the fridge and the butter in her handbag.

A similar expression is:

perdre la boule* – to go bonkers* or nuts*; to go off one's rocker*

Literally: to lose the ball

Je crois que ma mère perd la boule. Elle a déjà dix chats et maintenant elle veut un chien !

I think my mum's going off her rocker. She already has ten cats and now she wants a dog!

ⓘ *La boule* is a slang word for a head.

- ***mieux vaut prévenir que guérir (proverbe)*** – prevention is better than cure (proverb)

Literally: better worth prevent than cure

La vaccination est importante. Mieux vaut prévenir que guérir !
Vaccination is important. Prevention is better than cure!

- ***se mélanger les pieds*** ou ***les pédales*** ou ***les pinceaux*** ou ***les crayons*** – to get into a muddle

Literally: to mix up the feet *or* the pedals *or* the paintbrushes *or* the pencils

Mon grand-père souffre de la maladie d'Alzheimer et il a commencé à se mélanger les pinceaux.

My grandfather has Alzheimer's and he's started to get into a muddle.

Though *les pinceaux* are literally paintbrushes, *pinceaux* is a slang word for feet or legs, so the expression is just a variation of *se mélanger les jambes.*

Recently, *se mélanger les crayons* has become popular in speech and this has no doubt developed through the link with artists' materials, *pinceaux* leading to *crayons* - pencils.

- ***sucrer les fraises*** – to have a nervous tremble; to become senile

Literally: to sugar the strawberries

Si jamais un jour je commence à sucrer les fraises, je me fous en l'air !

If I ever I start to go senile, I'll do myself in!

Have you ever seen a person using a shaker to sprinkle sugar on a bowl of strawberries? The jerky movements needed to distribute the sugar evenly are reminiscent of the nervous trembling of someone with a condition such as Parkinson's. This joke (in very poor taste, admittedly!) is the origin of this expression.

Georges Planelles on his excellent website Expressio cites a source from 1901, a journalist and playwright, Aurélien Scholl, joking about an old soldier:

« *Cinquante années d'absinthe lui ont donné un tremblement tel que, lorsqu'il veut se verser à boire, le liquide secoué se répand comme une pluie autour du verre.*
- C'est désagréable, d'un côté, a dit le colonel ; mais, quand je prends la passoire avec du sucre en poudre... on peut voir combien cette infirmité devient précieuse pour sucrer les fraises. »

'Fifty years of absinthe have given him a tremor, such that, when he wants to pour himself something to drink, the shaken liquid spreads like rain about the glass.'

'It's unpleasant, on the one hand,' said the colonel, 'but when I take the shaker with the powdered sugar... one can see how this infirmity becomes valuable for sugaring the strawberries.'

It would be surprising to hear a young person using this expression. Older people are more likely to use this in a self-deprecating way.

- ***tomber dans les pommes*** * – to faint; to pass out

Literally: to fall in the apples

- ***rester dans les pommes*** * – to stay out cold; to remain unconscious

Literally: to stay in the apples

Catherine s'est cogné la tête contre une branche basse, et elle est restée dans les pommes pendant deux minutes.

Catherine hit her head on a low branch, and she was out cold for two minutes.

The origin of *être* or *tomber dans les pommes* is uncertain. It seems the most likely source is courtesy of the writer George Sand (1804-1876), who wrote in a letter to Madame Dupin that she was '*dans les pommes cuites*' meaning she was exhausted or 'done for', as in the expression *être cuit*.

Le Robert Dictionnaire historique de la langue française suggests a link with an older saying, *on abattrait cette muraille à coup de pommes cuites* - you could knock this wall down with blows from a cooked apple.

- ***tourner de l'œil*** – to faint; to pass out; to keel over

Literally: to turn of the eye

Le bar tournait, mon cœur palpitait, et j'ai fini par tourner de l'œil.

The bar was spinning, my heart was pounding, and I ended up passing out.

Originally, *tourner de l'œil* meant 'to die' but now it means only 'to pass out'.

Le sommeil – sleep

Taking an afternoon nap (*faire une sieste*) is not quite as widespread in France as it is in hotter European countries such as Spain. There are three types of siesta: *la micro-sieste*, lasting less than five minutes, *la sieste éclair*, generally ten to thirty minutes, and '*la sieste royale*' which lasts for more than one hour.

- **dormir** ou **coucher à la belle étoile** – to sleep under the stars

  Literally: to sleep *or* to spend the night at the beautiful star

  Je vais placer un morceau de bâche en plastique sous mon sac de couchage et je vais dormir à la belle étoile.

  I'm going to put a piece of plastic sheeting under my sleeping bag and I'm going to sleep under the stars.

According to Internaute.com, the expression *dormir à la belle étoile* used to be used ironically as if *La Belle Étoile* were the name of an inn (The Beautiful Star) and the ceiling above you the stars in the night sky.

- **dormir à poings fermés** – to sleep like a log

Literally: to sleep with fists closed

Le cambrioleur est entré dans la chambre à pas de loup, soucieux de ne pas faire de bruit, mais l'enfant dormait à poings fermés. Elle n'allait pas se réveiller facilement.

The burglar crept into the bedroom, anxious not to make a noise, but the child was sleeping like a log. She wasn't going to awaken easily.

- ***dormir comme un loir** ou **une marmotte** ou **une souche** ou **une bûche*** – to sleep like a log

Literally: to sleep like a dormouse *or* a marmot *or* a stump *or* a log

Je suis très jalouse de mon mari : il dort comme un loir, mais moi, je me réveille tous les matins à quatre heures.

I'm very jealous of my husband: he sleeps like a log, but I wake up every morning at 4am.

- ***dormir sur ses deux oreilles*** – to sleep soundly; to sleep safely (in one's bed)

Literally: to sleep on one's two ears

Je voulais arranger les choses avant de me coucher pour que je puisse dormir sur mes deux oreilles.

I wanted to sort things out before going to bed so that I could sleep soundly.

How can you sleep on two ears? Impossible! But if you could, you would certainly be sleeping soundly because you wouldn't hear anything. Maybe this expression has evolved because it has an opposite meaning to *ne dormir que d'un œil*, 'to sleep with one eye open' but its true origin is unknown.

- ***faire la grasse matinée*** – to have a lie in

Literally: to do the greasy morning

Le samedi je me lève rarement avant midi. J'adore faire la grasse matinée !

I rarely get up before midday on Saturdays. I love having a lie in!

Though you might wake up feeling rather greasy if you lie in bed for the whole morning, the word *gras* can also be translated as 'rich', 'abundant' or 'generous'. It may be this which is at the root of the expression.

- ***passer une nuit blanche*** – to have a sleepless night

Literally: to pass a white night

Excuse-moi si je m'endors dans mon fauteuil. J'ai passé une nuit blanche.

I'm sorry if I fall asleep in my armchair. I had a sleepless night.

The origins of this 18th century expression are not clear but the most likely is that it is simply the opposite of *la nuit noire*. Night is dark and is meant for sleeping; the opposite would imply a night without sleep, perhaps even spent with a light on.

Another likely possibility comes from St Petersburg in Russia, a place much frequented by the French aristocracy in the 18th century. In St Petersburg in summer, there is not much darkness at all at night because of its latitude, and parties would carry on right through the night. The Russian term, 'белые ночи', literally 'white nights', means 'nights without sleep'. It is likely that the French visitors of the 18th century brought back this Russian turn of phrase and it passed into the French language. There is still a White Nights Festival in St Petersburg where people go without sleep and enjoy a range of cultural events under the midnight sun. Similar festivals have popped up all over Europe. Paris has hosted a Nuit Blanche festival every October since 2002.

- *piquer du nez dans* ou *sur son assiette** – to nod off (during a meal); to hang one's head in shame

Literally: to sting of the nose in *or* on one's plate

Pendant le réveillon de Noël, le petit Pierre piqua du nez sur son assiette.

During the Christmas Eve meal, little Pierre nodded off.

- **s'endormir comme une masse** – to go out like a light; to fall asleep quickly

Literally: to fall asleep like a sledgehammer

J'ai pris un cachet et je me suis endormi comme une masse dix minutes plus tard.

I took a pill and I went out like a light ten minutes later.

La mort – death

Some of the greatest French men and women in history have been buried in the Paris mausoleum, *le Panthéon*, built in 1789 just before the French Revolution. Voltaire, Victor Hugo, Émile Zola, Jean Jacques Rousseau, Louis Braille, Alexandre Dumas, and Pierre and Marie Curie, were all buried there (Pierre and Marie Curie's coffins were lead-lined as their bodies were radioactive.)

When the rock and roll legend Johnny Hallyday died in 2017, there were calls for him to join the great and the good in the *Panthéon*. Almost a million people turned out to watch his funeral cortège travel down the Champs-Élysées to a memorial ceremony in the Église de la Madeleine, but he was finally laid to rest on the island of Saint-Barthélemy in the Caribbean, according to his final wishes.

- ***avoir un pied dans la tombe*** – to have one foot in the grave

Literally: to have one foot in the grave

Vous pensez peut-être que j'ai déjà un pied dans la tombe ? Alors, avant d'y passer, je vais vous montrer de quel bois je me chauffe !

You think maybe I've already got one foot in the grave? Well, before I pass on, I'm going to show you what I'm made of!

- ***ça sent le sapin**** – the end is near; he *or* she has one foot in the grave

Literally: it smells of fir *or* pine

Je ne veux pas avoir l'air d'être sans cœur, mais Oncle Gilbert a quatre-vingt-dix ans. Ça sent le sapin, non ?

I don't want to appear heartless, but Uncle Gilbert is ninety years old. He's got one foot in the grave, hasn't he?

Pine has long been used as a cheap wood for making coffins and therein lies the origin of this old expression which was first noted in 1694.

- ***casser sa pipe**** – to kick the bucket**; to snuff it**

Literally: to break one's pipe

Le vieux type qui habite plus bas dans la rue a cassé sa pipe hier. Une crise cardiaque, je crois.

The old bloke who lives down the road kicked the bucket yesterday. A heart attack, I think.

- ***faire le grand saut*** – to meet one's final hour

Literally: to do the big leap

Yanis est décédé ; après de longues souffrances patiemment endurées, il a fait le grand saut le 25 septembre.

Yanis has died; after much suffering patiently borne, he met his final hour on September 25th.

Quiz 7

1. « Marie-Agnès dort ?
– Oui, elle dort à ... »
a) *mains fermées.*
b) *poings fermés.*
c) *poêle fermé.*

2. *Nous aimons le dimanche parce que nous pouvons...*
a) *faire la grosse matinée.*
b) *faire la grasse matinée.*
c) *manger de la graisse toute la matinée.*

3. « Il est très vieux, son papy ?
– Oui, il a l'air d'avoir un pied dans ... »
a) *la chaussure.*
b) *la chaussette.*
c) *la tombe.*

4. *Tu es désorientée. Tu te mélanges les ...*
a) *pinceaux.*
b) *princes.*
c) *ponceaux.*

5. *J'espère ne pas ... ma pipe avant de me marier une troisième fois !*
a) *perdre*
b) *fumer*
c) *casser*

6. « Élizabeth est toujours vivante ?
– Non, elle a fait le grand ... pendant la nuit. »
a) *saut*
b) *seau*
c) *sot*

7. *Mon mari n'est pas insomniaque. Il s'endort toujours ...*
a) *en masse.*
b) *aux masses.*
c) *comme une masse.*

8. *Je serai contente quand ma fille sera de retour. Je pourrai dormir sur mes deux...*
a) *oreilles.*
b) *yeux.*
c) *joues.*

9. *Je l'aime d'amour mon Pépé ! Ça me rend triste, mais il commence un peu à sucrer ... !*
a) *les framboises*
b) *les fraises*
c) *les fruits*

10. *Mangez au moins cinq portions de fruits et légumes par jour ! Mieux vaut prévenir que ...*
a) *guérir.*
b) *gémir.*
c) *périr.*

11. *Maman et Papa ont une tente mais s'il continue à faire beau, moi, je vais dormir ...*
a) *à la belle étoile.*
b) *à l'étoile polaire.*
c) *à l'étoile filante.*

12. *Ma mère a essayé tous les traitements possibles mais sans succès. Elle sait que ça sent ...*
a) *le lapin.*
b) *la tarte Tatin.*
c) *le sapin.*

13. *La jeune fille était tellement fatiguée qu'elle ... sur son assiette.*
a) *s'est écrasé le nez*
b) *a piqué du nez*
c) *s'est mis les doigts dans le nez*

14. *Le sang a quitté son visage. J'ai cru qu'elle allait tourner ...*
a) *des yeux.*
b) *de l'oreille.*
c) *de l'œil.*

15. *Je n'ai pas encore fini mes devoirs mais je dois me coucher. Je n'ai plus les yeux ... trous.*
a) *dans les*
b) *à côté des*
c) *en face des*

16. *Je n'aime pas du tout les hôpitaux et j'ai une peur bleue de passer ... le billard.*
a) *devant*
b) *sur*
c) *sous*

17. *Où ai-je la tête ? Je perds ...*
a) *les pédales.*
b) *ma bicyclette.*
c) *mes pneus.*

18. *Tout d'un coup je me suis sentie mal et …*
a) *j'ai plongé dans les pommes.*
b) *j'ai mangé les pommes.*
c) *je suis tombée dans les pommes.*

19. *Je suis épuisée ! J'ai passé une nuit ...*
a) *noire.*
b) *claire.*
c) *blanche.*

20. *Après une journée très fatigante, Amal dormait comme…*
a) *la Loire.*
b) *le Loir.*
c) *un loir.*

Answers 7

1. b
2. b
3. c
4. a
5. c
6. a
7. c
8. a
9. b
10. a

11. a
12. c
13. b
14. c
15. c
16. b
17. a
18. c
19. c
20. c

CHAPTER 8

La mort (suite) – death (cont.)

Of all the most beautiful and poignant poems which have been written about death, my two favourite must be *'Demain, dès l'aube...'* by Victor Hugo (1856), which describes a visit to his daughter's grave, and *'Le dormeur du Val'*, written in 1870 by the poet Arthur Rimbaud at the age of 16 about a young soldier whose dead body lies incongruously surrounded by the beauties of nature. Here is *'Le Dormeur du Val'* and my translation.

Le dormeur du val

C'est un trou de verdure où chante une rivière,
Accrochant follement aux herbes des haillons
D'argent ; où le soleil, de la montagne fière,
Luit : c'est un petit val qui mousse de rayons.

Un soldat jeune, bouche ouverte, tête nue,
Et la nuque baignant dans le frais cresson bleu,
Dort ; il est étendu dans l'herbe, sous la nue,
Pâle dans son lit vert où la lumière pleut.

Les pieds dans les glaïeuls, il dort. Souriant comme
Sourirait un enfant malade, il fait un somme :
Nature, berce-le chaudement : il a froid.

Les parfums ne font pas frissonner sa narine ;
Il dort dans le soleil, la main sur sa poitrine,
Tranquille. Il a deux trous rouges au côté droit.

It is a pocket of green where sings a river
Wildly catching the grasses with rags
Of silver; where the sun, from the proud mountain,
Glows: it is a little valley bubbling with rays.

A soldier, young, mouth open, head bare,
And the nape of his neck bathing in the fresh blue watercress,
Is sleeping; he is lying in the grass, under the skies,
Pale in his green bed where the light rains down.

His feet in the gladioli, he sleeps. Smiling as
Would smile a sick child, he is dozing:
Nature, cradle him warmly: he is cold.

The scents do not make his nostrils quiver;
He is sleeping in the sun, his hand on his chest,
Tranquil. He has two red holes in his right side.

And having paused to reflect on this exquisite poem, let's get back to those French expressions!

- ***manger les pissenlits par la racine*** * – to be pushing up daisies*; to be dead and buried

Literally: to eat the dandelions by the root

« Je suis sûr d'avoir vu John Lennon ce matin !
  - Pas possible ! Il mange les pissenlits par la racine. »

'I'm sure I saw John Lennon this morning!'
'Not possible. He's pushing up daisies.'

- ***mourir de sa belle mort*** – to die a natural death

Literally: to die of one's beautiful death

Je voudrais mourir de ma belle mort dans mon sommeil à l'âge de cent ans.

I'd like to die a natural death in my sleep at the age of a hundred.

- ***passer l'arme à gauche**** – to kick the bucket**

Literally: to pass the weapon to left

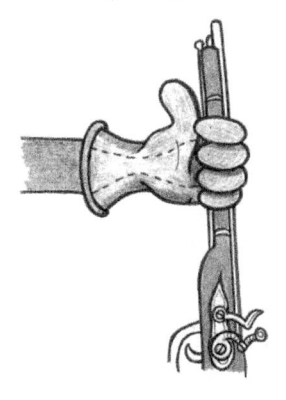

Avant de passer l'arme à gauche, je veux faire le tour du monde et m'amuser comme un fou sans penser aux autres.

Before I kick the bucket, I want to tour the world and have the time of my life without thinking about other people.

Rey suggests that this expression comes from the world of fencing. *Passer l'arme à gauche* means 'to be disarmed'. If you are disarmed, it is likely you are on the way to being killed!

Other origins are equally possible though. Expressio has several other suggestions too. Firstly, anything to do with the left has connotations of clumsiness or evil (the modern word for left is *gauche*, but this replaced the older word for left, *senestre*, which also meant 'sinister').

It is possible that the origin lies in the at-ease position of a soldier where his gun pointed down to the left.

Another possibility goes back to the Napoleonic Wars where soldiers needing to re-arm had to put their guns to the ground to the left of them and bend over them to fill them with powder and shot, thus making themselves vulnerable to enemy fire.

The final explanation comes from the Middle Ages from the times of heraldry. When two families were joined in marriage, their two emblems were put side by side on the coat of arms, the husband's on the right and the wife's on the left. If the husband died, his arms were passed over to the left-hand side of the coat of arms.

- ***rendre l'âme*** – to give up the ghost

Literally: to give back the soul

Au garage on m'a dit qu'une tête de bielle était coulée. Ma chère vieille bagnole a rendu l'âme !

At the garage I was told the big end had gone. My dear old banger has given up the ghost!

- ***tomber raide mort*** – to drop down dead

Literally: to fall stiff dead

Le père Girard est tombé raide mort dans la rue cet après-midi.

Old Girard dropped down dead in the street this afternoon.

La chance – luck

If you want to bet on the horses, you can go into any of the PMU outlets you can find everywhere in France (there were 12,500 of them in 2014). *Le Pari Mutuel Urbain* is the only operator authorised to accept bets on horseracing away from racecourses. Of course, you can now use a smartphone application to place a bet. *Un pari* is 'a bet' and *parier* is 'to bet'.

Gambling addiction (*l'accoutumance aux jeux de hasard* or *la dépendance au jeu*) is a growing problem in France. It is estimated that almost a million people are addicted to playing scratch card games (*les jeux de grattage*) and to the lottery (*la loterie*).

- **avoir du pot* ou du bol*** – to be lucky

Literally: to have some pot *or* bowl

Ça alors, tu as gagné du premier coup ! Tu as vraiment du pot !

Wow, you won straight off. You're really lucky!

Avoir du bol (1945) and *avoir du pot* (1926) have the same origin. They come from slang words for the anus or the backside! In the 19th century a range of words for receptacles such as *bol, pot, bock* and *bocal* all came to mean 'backside' in *argot*. (Was it the shape of the cheeks?) Also, with the invention of the car came the *pot d'échappement,* 'the exhaust pipe', out of which came noxious gases, a further link to the anus! So, in workers' slang 'to have some backside *or* anus' was 'to have some luck'. Why not!

ⓘ Two rather more vulgar, slang expressions along the same lines are:

> **avoir du cul***** – to be lucky

Literally: to have some bum*
and
> **avoir le cul*** bordé de nouilles** – to be very lucky

Literally: to have the bum* edged with noodles.

(If you do an internet search on this one, you will find some interesting images!)

- **c'est au petit bonheur (la chance)** – it's just the luck of the draw; it's pot luck; it's haphazard

Literally: it is to the small luck (the luck)

On ne peut pas choisir sa première affectation ; c'est au petit bonheur la chance.

You can't choose where your first posting will be; it's just pot luck.

✒ *Bonheur* means 'happiness' but also 'luck' or 'good fortune'. It comes from *bon heur, heur* meaning 'luck'.

- **c'est la faute à pas de chance** – it's just bad luck

Literally: it is the fault of no luck

À la suite des inondations qui ont touché le pays au mois de juin, devrait-on s'interroger sur le rôle de l'action humaine, ou est-ce la faute à pas de chance ?

Following the floods which affected the country in the month of June, should we be questioning the role of human activity, or is it just bad luck?

Le sport – sport

According to a Harris poll taken in 2017, when asked for their favourite sport, football (*le foot*) came out on top for the French. In second place was walking (*la marche/randonnée*) and in third place there was a tie between rugby (*le rugby*) and swimming (*la natation*). However, that did not mean that the respondents participated in those sports. When asked about the sports they took part in, walking was the most popular, followed by *le fitness/la musculation* (working out) and swimming.

Those who took part in sport at least once a week (6 out of 10 of those surveyed) on average spent 264 € per month.

- ***faire cavalier seul*** – to go it alone

Literally: to do lone rider

Personne ne veut se joindre à moi ? Alors, je ferai cavalier seul.

No-one wants to join me? Then I'll go it alone.

This expression does not come directly from the battlefield but from an early 19th century dance! The dance was called *un quadrille* and in one section of it the men danced alone like lone riders.

- **faire mouche** – to hit the bull's-eye; to score a bull's-eye; (figuratively) to score; to hit home; to hit a sensitive point

Literally: to make fly

Amel a lancé une boulette de papier sur son petit frère et elle a fait mouche !

Amel threw a ball of paper at her little brother and she hit bull's-eye!

The very centre of an archery target is called *la mouche* in French. It is black and is the size of a big fat fly.

- **gagner** ou **arriver dans un fauteuil*** – to romp home; to win easily

Literally: to win *or* to arrive in an armchair

Avec plus de cinq secondes d'avance sur les autres coureurs, Marc Sarreau a gagné dans un fauteuil.

With more than five seconds on the other cyclists, Marc Sarreau romped home.

- ***gagner haut la main*** – to win hands down

Literally: to win high the hand

Arrête de tricher. Je l'ai gagné haut la main !

Stop cheating. I won it hands down!

- ***gagner les doigts dans le nez**** – to win easily *or* hands down

Literally: to win (the) fingers in the nose

Usain Bolt explosa le record du monde du 100 mètres, gagnant les doigts dans le nez.

Usain Bolt exploded the world 100 metre record, winning hands down.

This expression was first noted in 1912 in the context of horse racing. Imagine a jockey who is winning so comfortably that he has time to pick his nose nonchalantly while crossing the finishing line!

- ***mettre* ou *taper (en plein) dans le mille*** – to hit a bull's-eye; to be bang on target*; to hit the nail on the head

Literally: to put *or* to hit (fully) in the thousand

Je viens d'ouvrir ton magnifique colis. Merci mille fois ! Tu as tapé dans le mille ! J'adore tout !

I've just opened your wonderful parcel. Thank you so much! You were bang on target! I love everything!

According to Rey, *le jeu de tonneau* – the barrel game (also called *le jeu de grenouille* – the frog game) is the origin of this expression. Popular in the late-19th century, this game would have been a common sight at a country fair. It consisted of a wooden plank with holes, sitting on top of a barrel. In the middle of the plank was fixed a metal frog with a large mouth. A player would try to throw pucks from a distance of around three metres into any of the holes to gain points. The highest that one could score was 1000 if the puck went into the frog's mouth.

- ***mettre quelqu'un KO**** – to knock somebody out *or* for six

Literally: to put somebody KO

Le choc l'a mis KO.

The blow knocked him for six.

The French adopted the English boxing expression 'knock-out' but then shortened it to KO pronounced using the French alphabet. Consequently, an English person would not recognise the expression. They have been using this abbreviation since 1909 and have been confusing English speakers with it ever since!

ⓘ Notice (just to add to the fun) that *KO* is pronounced the same way as the French word for chaos: *chaos*.

- **nager comme un fer à repasser*** – to swim like a brick

Literally: to swim like an iron

J'ai eu dix semaines de leçons, mais je nage toujours comme un fer à repasser.

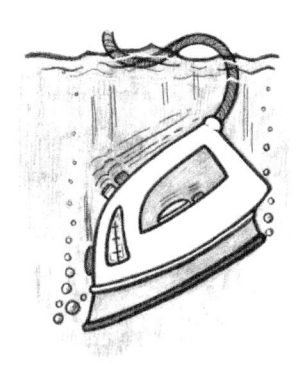

I've had ten weeks of lessons, but I still swim like a brick.

- **saisir la balle au bond** – to seize the opportunity (while the going is good); to be sharp-witted in discussion

Literally: to seize the ball at the bounce

J'ai remarqué que la patronne était de bonne humeur, donc j'ai saisi la balle au bond et je lui ai demandé un jour de congé.

I noticed the boss was in a good mood, so I seized the opportunity and asked her for a day off.

According to the *Comité Français de Courte-Paume*, this expression came from the *jeu de paume* or real/royal tennis and it meant 'to catch the ball before the bounce'. You must be really fast to be able to do this.

- ***se mettre en jambe(s)**** – to warm up

Literally: to put oneself in leg(s)

Noah s'est mis à courir tout de suite, mais moi, je tenais à faire d'abord quelques exercices d'étirement, histoire de me mettre en jambes.

Noah started running straight away, but I was keen to do some stretching exercises first just to warm up.

ⓘ It is not only in sport that this expression is used. For example, a maths teacher might start a class with a warm up exercise: « *On va faire un petit exercice de calcul mental pour nous mettre en jambes* » – 'we are going to do a little mental arithmetic exercise to get us warmed up'. A synonym for *se mettre en jambe(s)* is the more common *s'échauffer*. The noun 'a warm up' is *'une mise en jambes'* but you can also use *'un échauffement'*.

- ***tirer** ou **retirer son épingle du jeu*** – to play one's game well; to extricate oneself (without losing money)

Literally: to pull *or* to remove one's pin from the game

Lorsque la Bourse des valeurs tombait et alors que tout le monde perdait beaucoup d'argent, Xavier a réussi à très bien tirer son épingle du jeu.

When the Stock Exchange was falling and everybody was losing lots of money, Xavier managed to extricate himself well.

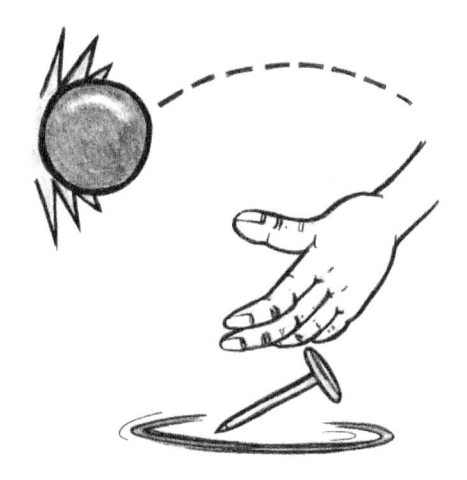

Expressio gives some very interesting historical details to help us understand this expression. Firstly, the expression goes back to the 16th century and probably relates to a child's game of the 15th century. The most likely one is a game where a ball would be thrown against a wall, and in the time it took the ball to bounce back, the child would bend down to pick up a pin from a circle drawn on the ground.

However, when we look at the wider meanings of some of the words, we can understand the expression more fully. *Tirer* not only means 'to pull' but is used in other related expressions such as **se tirer d'affaire**. *'Il s'est tiré d'affaire'* means 'he pulled through' after an illness or 'he got out of a tight spot'. *Jeu* not only means 'game' but is used in expressions such as **être en jeu** (to be at stake) and **mettre tout en jeu** (to risk everything).

Also, in the 16th century, *épingle* not only meant 'pin' but also had the sexual meaning of 'penis' (like 'prick' in English). In the days before the pill had been invented, it was a good idea for a young man to withdraw early before it ended up costing him a lot of money!

- **y a pas photo*** – there's no question about it; there's no competition; there's a big difference

Literally: there isn't photo

Entre les deux candidats y a pas photo.

There's no competition between the two candidates.

Shortened from *il n'y a pas photo*, this expression comes from horseracing in the 1980s. If a photo-finish is needed, *il y a photo*, but if the distance between the winner and the runner-up is great, *y a pas photo.*

If you search for this expression on the internet and even in some dictionaries, you are highly likely to find it written as '*y'a pas photo*' with an apostrophe. However, as there is no letter missing after the *y*, no apostrophe is needed. According to @Projet_Voltaire, '*il n'y a jamais d'apostrophe après le « y »*'. It is not only in English that there are apostrophe wars!

Quiz 8

1. *Je ne suis pas très doué au tennis. Mon frère a gagné …*
a) *la main haute.*
b) *les mains hautes.*
c) *haut la main.*

2. *Le discours du président sur l'économie a fait … chez les banquiers.*
a) *mouche*
b) *abeille*
c) *guêpe*

3. *Elle n'a pas perdu d'argent. Elle a réussi à très bien tirer … du jeu.*
a) *son épingle*
b) *son aiguille*
c) *son clou*

4. *J'espère ne pas passer l'arme … avant l'âge de quatre-vingt-dix-neuf ans.*
a) *à droite*
b) *à gauche*
c) *tout droit*

5. *J'ai quitté la gare cinq minutes avant l'explosion. J'ai eu …*
a) *du pot.*
b) *deux pots.*
c) *un pot.*

6. *Il a l'esprit vif. Quand je parle avec lui, il saisit … au bond.*
a) *la balle*
b) *la bulle*
c) *la belle*

7. *Il n'y a pas de vraie sélection. C'est au … la chance.*
a) *petit bonheur*
b) *bonheur*
c) *plus de bonheur*

8. *Ma belle-mère n'a pas souffert. Elle est morte de sa … mort hier soir.*
a) *jolie*
b) *petite*
c) *belle*

9. *Avant de commencer un marathon, il est important de se mettre …*
a) *en jambes.*
b) *sur pied.*
c) *à pied.*

10. *Romane a gagné. Y a pas …*
a) *dodo.*
b) *photo.*
c) *logo.*

11. *L'électricien a reçu une décharge électrique et il est tombé…*
a) *droit mort.*
b) *raide mort.*
c) *mort raide.*

12. *L'ouragan a tout détruit, et je ne pouvais rien y faire. C'était la faute à … !*
a) *pas de ça*
b) *pas de deux*
c) *pas de chance*

13. *Lui qui était un si bon jardinier, eh bien maintenant, le pauvre, il mange les … par la racine !*
a) *marguerites*
b) *pissenlits*
c) *coquelicots*

14. *C'est la meilleure sprinteuse française. Elle va gagner les doigts dans …*
a) *l'oreille.*
b) *le nez.*
c) *l'œil.*

15. *Mon pauvre chien, Snoopy, a rendu … hier.*
a) *l'âme*
b) *l'arme*
c) *la larme*

16. *Personne ne voulait fonder un commerce avec moi donc j'ai …*
a) *fait cavalier seul.*
b) *fait du cheval seul.*
c) *acheté un cheval.*

17. *Mon compagnon nage bien mais moi, je nage comme …*
a) *une planche à repasser.*
b) *un lave-linge.*
c) *un fer à repasser.*

18. *Il est de loin le meilleur coureur. Il va gagner dans…*
a) *une chaise.*
b) *un fauteuil.*
c) *une baignoire.*

19. *Il l'a frappé d'une telle force qu'il l'a mis …*
a) *LOL.*
b) *KO.*
c) *OK.*

20. *Tu as tapé dans … avec ta première réponse.*
a) *le mille.*
b) *le milieu.*
c) *un millier.*

Answers 8

1. c
2. a
3. a
4. b
5. a
6. a
7. a
8. c
9. a
10. b

11. b
12. c
13. b
14. b
15. a
16. a
17. c
18. b
19. b
20. a

CHAPTER 9

L'attirance et l'apparence – attraction and appearance

One of my favourite francophone poets is the late Esther Granek, a Belgian-Israeli who survived the Holocaust and went on to write five collections of poetry. To get us in the mood for this chapter, here is her poem *'Coloris'* (Colours) taken from her collection *Portraits et chansons sans retouches*, 1976.

En teintes folles, en demi-tons,
dans la lumière qui resplendit,
tes cheveux sont couleur de miel
et tes yeux sont couleur de ciel
tes lèvres sont couleur de vie
et sur ta peau d'un blond roussi
le soleil a fait un semis
de mille jolies taches de son.

And my rather less poetic translation:

In mad shades, in half-tones,
In the light which shines,
your hair is the colour of honey
and your eyes are the colour of the sky
your lips are the colour of life
and on your tanned blond skin
the sun has sown
a thousand pretty freckles.

- **à poil**** – stark naked

Literally: at hair

Océane a crié quand je me suis trompé de porte et que je l'ai trouvée à poil.

Océane screamed when I got the wrong door and I found her stark naked.

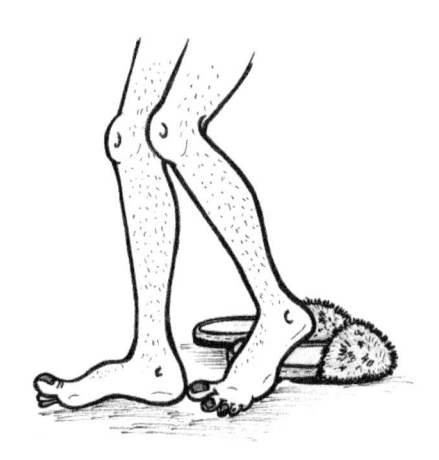

- **avoir** ou **faire une partie de jambes en l'air**** – to have a roll in the hay*; to have some hanky-panky*; to bonk**

Literally: to have *or* to do a game of legs in the air

« *Quand tu sors avec Paul, vous parlez beaucoup ?*
   - *Parler ? Non ! Tout ce qui l'intéresse, c'est une partie de jambes en l'air !* »

'When you go out with Paul, do you talk much?'
'Talk? No! All he's interested in is hanky-panky.'

- ***avoir un œil qui dit merde*** à l'autre*** – to squint; to be cross-eyed

Literally: to have one eye which says shit to the other

Comme il avait un œil qui disait merde à l'autre, je ne savais pas trop s'il s'adressait à moi ou à mon amie !

As he was cross-eyed, I didn't really know if he was talking to me or my friend!

If you prefer to be less vulgar, you could use this alternative:

avoir un œil qui joue au billard et l'autre qui compte les points

Literally: to have one eye which is playing billiards *or* pool and the other which is counting the points

(i) If you want to be boring and avoid colourful metaphors, then simply use the verb *loucher*, 'to squint'. *Un strabisme* is 'a squint'.

- ***bas les pattes !**** – keep your hands to yourself

Literally: down the paws

Ne me touche pas avant d'avoir pris une douche. Bas les pattes, j'ai dit !

Don't touch me until you've showered. Hands off, I said!

(i) *'Bas les pattes!'* is also the command you would give to a dog: 'Down!'

- ***battre la chamade*** – to pound; to beat wildly

Literally: to beat the drum signal

Quand Patrice l'a embrassée pour la première fois, son cœur battait la chamade.

When Patrice kissed her for the first time, her heart was beating wildly.

La chamade is not used widely in French apart from in this figurative expression dating from the 19th century, which is borrowed from the military. *La chamade* was the drum and trumpet signal announcing the desire to parley.

Not surprisingly, the expression *battre la chamade* has been used in many song lyrics over the ages. One such example is in the classic *chanson* '*Le cœur volcan*' sung by Julien Clerc with lyrics by Étienne Roda-Gil:

« *Comme un volcan devenu vieux*
Mon cœur bat lentement la chamade.
La lave tiède de tes yeux
Coule dans mes veines malades. »

'Like a volcano become old
My heart pounds slowly.
The tepid lava of your eyes
Flows in my sick veins.'

(It sounds better in French!)

- ***beau*** ou ***belle à croquer*** – as pretty as a picture; good enough to eat

Literally: beautiful to sketch *or* crunch

Rachida est belle à croquer dans sa nouvelle robe.

Rachida is as pretty as a picture in her new dress.

The two meanings of *croquer* which interest us here are 'to sketch' and 'to crunch/bite into'. It is the former which is the likely origin of the expression *belle/jolie à croquer*; that is, 'she looks good enough to make you want to sketch her'. However, the second meaning no doubt added a touch of eroticism which made the expression such a good one.

- **dans le plus simple appareil (humoristique)** – in one's birthday suit (humorous) *or* in the altogether; naked *or* very nearly naked

Literally: in the simplest apparatus

Vanessa s'est déshabillée sur la rive et s'est baignée dans le plus simple appareil.

Vanessa undressed on the shore and bathed in the altogether.

The verb *appareiller* comes from the Latin, *apparere*, meaning 'to prepare'. The noun *appareil* which came from this used to have the meaning in the 12th century of 'preparation' rather than 'apparatus'. It took on the meaning of 'appearance in regalia' because of the long preparations required to dress for a ceremony.

In the expression *dans le plus simple appareil*, what we have is an apparent contradiction in the two ideas: being simple and spending a long time getting ready.

ⓘ Corneille used this expression to great effect in his play *Britannicus* (1669). In Act II, Scene 2, Néron, who is in love with Junie, describes her thus:

« *Excité d'un désir curieux,*
Cette nuit je l'ai vue arriver en ces lieux,
Triste, levant au ciel ses yeux mouillés de larmes,
Qui brillaient au travers des flambeaux et des armes,
Belle, sans ornement, dans le simple appareil
D'une beauté qu'on vient d'arracher au sommeil. »

Thanks to Timberlake Wertenbaker, we have this excellent translation:

'It was curiosity–
I saw her come to the palace last night.
She lifted her tear-filled eyes to the skies,
tears that glinted more brightly than weapons, flames–
Lovely, without ornaments, and simply
dressed with the beauty of one still asleep.'

- ***elle lui a tapé dans l'œil**** – he fancied her*; she piqued his interest; she caught his eye

Literally: she has hit him in the eye

Quand Charlotte est apparue dans sa petite robe en dentelle noire transparente, elle a tapé dans l'œil de Florian.

When Charlotte appeared wearing a transparent little black lace dress, she took Florian's fancy.

ⓘ *Taper dans l'œil* is often used in sports reporting. For example: *Le jeune attaquant a déjà tapé dans l'œil des recruteurs* – the young attacker has already caught the eye of the scouts.

❗ *Taper dans l'œil* should not be confused with the adjective *tape-à-l'œil* which means 'flashy' or 'showy'.

- **en tout bien tout honneur** – above board; in all innocence

Literally: in all good all honour

Il ne restait plus dans l'hôtel qu'une chambre avec un lit double. Ils l'ont prise en tout bien tout honneur.

There was only one room left in the hotel, which had a double bed. They took it in all innocence.

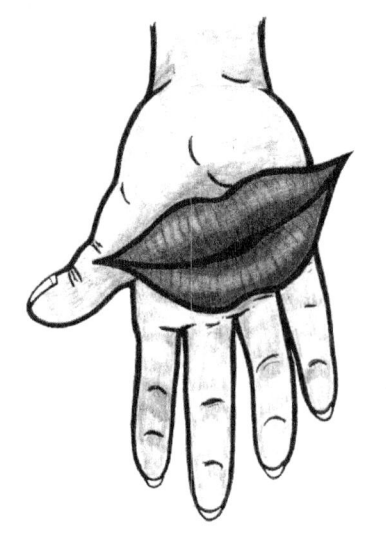

- **envoyer un baiser de la main** – to blow a kiss

Literally: to send a kiss from the hand

En démarrant, je lui ai envoyé un baiser de la main.

As I moved off, I blew her a kiss.

- ***habillé(e)* ou *ficelé(e)* ou *fagoté(e) comme l'as de pique*** – dressed any old how

Literally: dressed *or* tied up *or* rigged out like the ace of spades

On sait toujours si Béthanie a le cafard parce qu'elle s'habille alors comme l'as de pique.

You always know if Béthanie has got the blues because she dresses any old how.

If you look at the ace of spades in a pack of cards, you won't see an image of a person: there is only the spades symbol. So where did the expression come from? In the 19th century, to say someone was dressed *comme l'as de pique* was very insulting. The parson's nose of a chicken, its anus, is similar in shape to the ace of spades, and so *as de pique* in French slang meant *trou de cul* or 'asshole'!

Back in the 17th century, the expression *as de pique* already meant 'silly' (Molière used it in that sense) and it is possible that in speech it already carried the sense of 'asshole'.

These days it has dropped the association with the backside and is just used to mean that someone is lacking in taste in their choice of clothing.

- ***joli(e) comme un cœur*** – as pretty as a picture

Literally: pretty as a heart

Soraya est jolie comme un cœur avec sa nouvelle coiffure.

Soraya is as pretty as a picture with her new hairstyle.

- ***maigre comme un clou*** – as thin as a rake

Literally: thin as a nail

Inès veut être maigre comme un clou pour devenir mannequin. C'est malsain !

Inès wants to be as thin as a rake so she can become a model. It's unhealthy!

- ***maquillé(e) comme un camion volé**** ou ***une voiture volée**** – wearing an excessive amount of makeup

Literally: made-up like a stolen lorry *or* a stolen car

Ma belle-sœur, elle passe des heures à appliquer du faux bronzage, du fond de teint, du blush, du fard à paupières, du mascara, du rouge à lèvres. Elle est toujours maquillée comme un camion volé !

My sister-in-law, she spends hours putting on fake tan, foundation, blusher, eye-shadow, mascara, lipstick. She always wears an excessive amount of makeup!

If you steal a lorry, you don't want it to be recognised, so it is a good idea to get it resprayed with a new coat of paint before putting it back on the road. Sometimes it is hard to recognise the person under all the layers of makeup, so this can be a very apt expression!

In the same vein, you might hear this variation:

> **on dirait qu'elle** ou **qu'il a un pot de peinture sur le visage** ou **la tête** – she *or* he is wearing far too much makeup

Literally: one would say that she *or* he has a pot of paint on the face *or* the head

Or: **c'est un vrai pot de peinture !**

Literally: she *or* he is a real paint pot!

- **moche comme un pou*** – as ugly as sin; a face like the back of a bus

Literally: ugly as a louse

Je me sens moche comme un pou. Je vais m'offrir un relooking !

I feel as ugly as sin. I'm going to treat myself to a make-over!

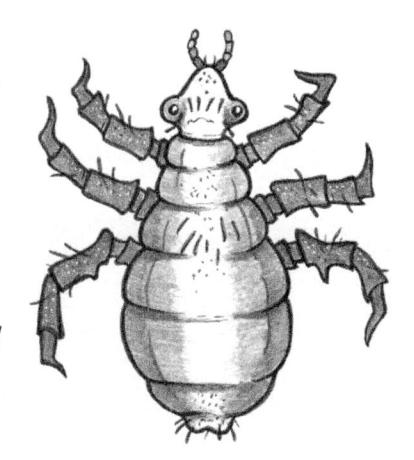

Why choose a louse to describe ugliness rather than any other insect? Planelles suggests that it was the idea of being louse-ridden that filled people with disgust, and which made the image so effective.

- ***nu(e) comme un ver*** – stark naked

  Literally: naked as a worm

  J'ai piqué un fard quand je me suis rendu compte que j'étais nu comme un ver.

  I went bright red when I realised that I was stark naked.

- ***rouler un patin*** ou ***une pelle** à quelqu'un*** – to give somebody a French kiss

  Literally: to roll a skate or a shovel to somebody

« Téo s'est bien amusé hier soir ?
– Bien évidemment ! Je l'ai vu rouler un patin à Gabia ! »

'Did Téo enjoy himself last night?'
'Obviously he did! I saw him giving Gabia a French kiss!'

The most likely origin of the slang expression *rouler un patin* is a distortion of *rouler à patin*, to roller-skate, the expression first being noted in 1927 when roller-skating had just become fashionable. A less appealing, possible origin is *une pattemouille*, a damp cloth.

Georges Planelles also writes of a feasible link to the 20th century slang verb *patiner* meaning 'to caress a sensitive part of the body to cause sexual excitement'.

The origin of *rouler une pelle*, rolling a shovel, is not clear, but there is a likely link to the shape of the tongue.

- **se coiffer avec un pétard*** – to have scruffy hair

Literally: to do one's hair with a firecracker

Elle fait bien son boulot, mais elle devrait faire plus d'effort côté apparence ; il y a des jours où on dirait qu'elle s'est coiffée avec un pétard.

She does her job well, but she should make more of an effort appearance-wise; some days her hair looks really scruffy.

- ***se mettre sur son trente et un*** * – to be dressed to kill; to get dressed up to the nines; to dress one's best

Literally: to put oneself on one's 31

Je sors avec Jean-Luc ce soir. Il me faudra trois heures pour me mettre sur mon trente et un.

I've got a date with Jean-Luc this evening. I'll need three hours to get dressed to kill.

No-one really knows the true origin of this expression though many possibilities have been suggested to do with card games, military uniforms, superior quality fabric named *trentain* and other earlier expressions such as *se mettre sur son trente-six*.

Le Robert Dictionnaire historique de la langue française suggests that it might be to do with 31 being one more than the normal length of month, so suggesting superiority. Who knows!

- ***tiré à quatre épingles*** – dressed up to the nines; (too) smartly dressed

Literally: pulled to four pins

Békir était tiré à quatre épingles, les cheveux soigneusement peignés en arrière, dans un costume impeccable, et portant une cravate parfaitement nouée.

Békir was smartly dressed; his hair was carefully combed back, and he was wearing a suit with a perfectly knotted tie.

From the 16th century, people wearing well-adjusted clothes were said to be *bien tiré*. A piece of fabric, when stretched and pinned in all four corners, would be without creases. When this expression was used in the 17th and 18th centuries, it meant that the person was dressed with artistry and symmetry. Nowadays if you say someone is *tiré à quatre épingles*, you might be suggesting that someone is perhaps too neatly dressed.

Quiz 9

1. *Il l'a accompagnée chez elle …*
a) *en tout bien tout honneur.*
b) *en tout honneur tout bien.*
c) *en tout bon tout honneur.*

2. *Je sors avec Hugo ce soir. Je vais me mettre sur mon trente …*
a) *-deux.*
b) *-six.*
c) *et un.*

3. *Ma fille aînée préfère le look naturel, mais la cadette est toujours maquillée comme …*
a) *un voleur.*
b) *un camion volé.*
c) *un canard volé.*

4. *« Qu'est-ce qu'elle portait quand elle sortait de la salle de bains ?*
– Elle était dans le plus simple … ! »
a) *appareil*
b) *apparence*
c) *apparition*

5. *Je suis sortie avec Jules hier soir et il m'a roulé … Beurk ! J'aime pas ça !*
a) *un skate.*
b) *un patin.*
c) *un vélo.*

6. *Tu es couvert d'huile. Bas … !*
a) *la pâte*
b) *le pâté*
c) *les pattes*

7. *Quand je quitte ma femme à l'aéroport, je lui envoie … de la main.*
a) *une bouteille*
b) *un bouquet*
c) *un baiser*

8. *Quand tu es nu(e), tu es …*
a) *à poil.*
b) *à cheveu.*
c) *à cheval.*

9. *J'ai enlevé mes vêtements. Je suis …*
a) *nu comme un ver vert.*
b) *nu comme un ver.*
c) *nu comme un verre.*

10. *Le jour de son mariage, elle était belle à …*
a) *croquer.*
b) *dessiner.*
c) *cracher.*

11. *Tu t'es fait couper les cheveux ! Tu es jolie comme …*
a) *du beurre.*
b) *un cœur.*
c) *la peur.*

12. *Je me sens débraillé à côté de lui qui est toujours tiré à ... épingles.*
a) *trente-six*
b) *dix*
c) *quatre*

13. *Marie-Laure mange comme un oiseau et elle est maigre comme ...*
a) *un râteau.*
b) *un clou.*
c) *un marteau.*

14. *Raphaël va rarement chez le coiffeur et on dirait qu'il se coiffe avec ...*
a) *une fusée.*
b) *une chandelle romaine.*
c) *un pétard.*

15. *Tu te souviens de Mélissa, celle qui avait un œil qui disait ... à l'autre ?*
a) *merde*
b) *merci*
c) *bonjour*

16. *L'homme de tes rêves ou la femme de tes rêves t'embrasse. Ton cœur ...*
a) *bat la trompette.*
b) *bat le chameau.*
c) *bat la chamade.*

17. *À sa naissance elle était moche comme ...*
a) *un pou.*
b) *une puce.*
c) *une poupée.*

18. *Jules t'a offert un verre ? Tiens, tu lui as tapé dans ... !*
a) *les yeux*
b) *la bouche*
c) *l'œil*

19. *Mon oncle ne s'intéresse pas du tout aux vêtements et il est toujours habillé comme l'as de ...*
a) *trèfle.*
b) *pique.*
c) *carreau.*

20. *Le vieil homme est mort subitement pendant une partie de ... en l'air avec sa jeune maîtresse.*
a) *jambes*
b) *pieds*
c) *mains*

Answers 9

1.	a	11.	b
2.	c	12.	c
3.	b	13.	b
4.	a	14.	c
5.	b	15.	a
6.	c	16.	c
7.	c	17.	a
8.	a	18.	c
9.	b	19.	b
10.	a	20.	a

CHAPTER 10

L'amour, le mariage et l'amitié – love, marriage and friendship

There is an extraordinary French reality television programme which blows the western tradition of courtship and marriage out of the water and replaces it with a 21st century version. It is called *"Mariés au premier regard"* (Married at First Sight). In each of the series, scientists match up six couples whom they believe to be compatible, and the couples see each other for the first time only when they are standing in front of the mayor on their wedding day and must decide on the spot whether they will say, *"Oui"* or *"Non, merci !"*. Cameras then follow them through the next few weeks until the day of a final meeting with the experts when they must decide if they would like to remain married or would prefer to divorce. Amazingly, some of these young couples withstand the pressure of intense media interest and do find true love. Not so surprisingly, most of them do not.

You can find this programme on 6Play or on YouTube. You will no doubt watch it because it will be excellent practice for your French, but beware, you might well be sucked into the dubious world of reality TV and (like the author of this book – much to her shame) be hooked!

l'amour rend aveugle ; l'amour est aveugle (proverbe) – love is blind (proverb)

Literally: the love makes blind; the love is blind

Ça fait quatre ans déjà que mon fils vit avec cette menteuse sournoise, mais il ne voit pas sa vraie nature. On dit que l'amour rend aveugle !

It's been four years now that my son has been living with that devious liar, but he can't see her true character. They say that love is blind!

This is an expression which goes back to Antiquity.

- ***avoir élevé* ou *gardé les cochons ensemble*** – to have been close since childhood; to be old pals

Literally: to have raised *or* kept the pigs together

« *Pourquoi est-ce que tu ne demanderais pas de l'aide à Monsieur le maire ? Tu le connais, n'est-ce pas ?*

- *Et s'il me répondait qu'on n'a pas élevé les cochons ensemble ? Je n'oserais pas !* »

'Why not ask the mayor for help. You know him, don't you?'

'And what if he replied that we're not old pals? I wouldn't dare!'

This expression is usually used in the negative form.

- ***avoir le béguin pour quelqu'un*** – to have a crush on somebody

Literally: to have the 14th century woman's headgear for somebody

Je t'ai vue le regarder de tes yeux de biche. Tu as le béguin pour lui, hein ?

I've seen you looking at him with your doe eyes. You've got a crush on him, haven't you!

Un béguin was originally the name for the headgear worn by the *béguine* religious order of the 14th century. By extension it became the name for a woman's headgear and for that of a small baby. Small babies' hats often fall down over their eyes so they can't see clearly. Perhaps this lack of clear vision is the basis for this expression.

There used to be a parallel expression, *être coiffé de quelqu'un,* which meant 'to be at somebody's mercy' or 'to be made powerless or blind by somebody' (*coiffer* literally means 'to put on a hat' or 'to do somebody's hair', and if somebody puts a hat on you, they might be thought to be dominating you).

Another possibility is that *avoir le béguin* derived from the 16th century expression which is no longer used, *avoir le béguin à l'envers,* 'to have the hat back-to-front' which meant 'to have a troubled head'.

One way or another, the expression has something to do with hats, not seeing clearly, and having daft ideas!

The expression *avoir le béguin pour quelqu'un* is similar to another hat-related expression, **(se) toquer de quelqu'un / quelque chose** (*une toque* being a fur hat) which also means 'to go crazy over somebody or something'. We might translate them both as 'to lose one's head over somebody or something'.

- ***avoir le coup de foudre pour quelqu'un*** – to fall head over heels in love with somebody

Literally: to have the lightning strike for somebody

- ***ce fut le coup de foudre*** – it was love at first sight

Literally: it was the lightning strike

Quand j'ai repéré ta maman aux noces de ta Tante Émilie, j'ai eu le coup de foudre, et trois semaines plus tard nous nous sommes mariés.

When I spotted your mum at your Aunt Emilie's wedding, I fell head over heels in love with her, and three weeks later we got married.

- ***avoir*** ou ***être un cœur d'artichaut*** – to be soft-hearted and fall in love easily

Literally: to have *or* to be an artichoke heart

L'année dernière Anaïs est tombée amoureuse du facteur, puis du boucher, et ensuite de son prof d'anglais. C'est un cœur d'artichaut !

Last year Anaïs fell in love with the postman, then the butcher, and then her English teacher. She falls in love with every man she meets!

Dating back to the late 19th century, this expression comes from the proverb '*cœur d'artichaut, une feuille pour tout le monde*' – 'artichoke heart, a leaf for everyone'. An artichoke has a tender heart, and has leaves which are pulled off to be nibbled. Someone with a soft heart might fall in love as many times as the number of leaves on an artichoke.

- ***avoir un fil à la patte**** – to be tied down

Literally: to have a cord on the paw

Depuis la naissance de ses jumeaux, Dylane ne sort plus avec ses copains. Il a maintenant un fil à la patte.

Since the birth of his twins, Dylane doesn't go out with his mates any more. He's tied down now.

- ***un bourreau des cœurs*** – a lady-killer *or* a heart-breaker; a fast worker

Literally: an executioner of the hearts

Il est toujours en train de courir après les filles puis il les quitte brutalement. C'est un bourreau des cœurs.

He's always running after the girls then he ditches them. He's a real heart-breaker.

- **enterrer sa vie de garçon** – to have a stag party

Literally: to bury one's boy's life

- **enterrer sa vie de jeune fille** – to have a hen party

Literally: to bury one's girl's life

- **enterrer sa vie de célibataire** – to have a stag or hen party

Literally: to bury one's life as a single person

Une semaine avant le jour de son mariage, Lucas est parti à Prague avec ses copains pour enterrer sa vie de garçon.

A week before his wedding day, Lucas went away to Prague with his mates for a stag do.

- **être aux petits soins pour quelqu'un** – to dance attendance on somebody; to wait on somebody hand and foot

Literally: to be at the little cares for somebody

Papa a de la chance. Maman est toujours aux petits soins pour lui.

Dad is lucky. Mum is always waiting on him hand and foot.

- **être comme cul et chemise avec quelqu'un*** – to be as thick as thieves with somebody

Literally: to be as bum and shirt with somebody

Je n'ai jamais vu Jérôme sans son frère. Ils sont comme cul et chemise.

I've never seen Jérôme without his brother. They're as thick as thieves.

This expression has evolved from an earlier one from the 17th century: *ce sont deux culs dans une chemise*, 'they are two bums in one shirt' or *ce n'est qu'un cul et une chemise*, 'it is only one bum and one shirt'. You can't get much closer than that!

- **être copains comme cochons*** – to be great buddies

Literally: to be mates like pigs

Gaston et Sacha sont copains comme cochons.

Gaston and Sacha are great buddies.

Surprisingly, the origin of this rather quaint expression has nothing to do with pigs! According to Georges Planelles, the word *cochon* in this expression came from an older word, *soçon*, which meant 'friend' or 'associate' from the Latin *socius*. In the 16th century the expression was *camarades comme cochons*, and in the 18th century *camarades* changed to *amis* before finally in the 19th century becoming *copains*.

être raide dingue de quelqu'un* – to be completely crazy about somebody

Literally: to be stiff mad of somebody

Tu sais que je suis raide dingue de toi depuis le moment où j'ai posé les yeux sur toi de l'autre côté de la piste de danse.

You know I've been completely crazy about you since the moment I clapped eyes on you across the dance floor.

- **M'aime-t-il** ou **M'aime-t-elle ? Un peu, beaucoup, passionnément, à la folie, pas du tout** – He loves me, he loves me not; she loves me, she loves me not.

Literally: Does he *or* she love me? A little, a lot, passionately, madly, not at all

Nora cueillit une marguerite dans l'herbe et commença à l'effeuiller.

« M'aime-t-il ? Un peu, beaucoup, passionnément, à la folie, pas du tout, un peu, beaucoup, passionnément… À la folie ! »

Nora picked a daisy from the grass and started to pluck the petals.

'He loves me, he loves me not, he loves me, he loves me not, he loves me, he loves me not, he loves me, he loves me not… he loves me!'

This little game of plucking a daisy one petal at a time to see whether you are loved or not is found in many cultures. In the English game, the odds are only 50-50 but the French formula gives you much more chance of being loved at least a little!

ⓘ Do you know the rapper Mc Solaar? Here are a few lines from his song *'Caroline'*:
« J'étais cool, assis sur un banc, c'était au printemps
Ils cueillent une marguerite, ce sont deux amants
Overdose de douceur, ils jouent comme des enfants
Je t'aime un peu, beaucoup, à la folie, passionnément. »

'I was cool, sitting on a bench, it was in the spring
They pick a daisy, they are two lovers
Overdose of sweetness, they play like children
I love you a little, a lot, madly, passionately.'

- **ne pas être au beau fixe** –
  (relationships) to be a bit strained

Literally: not to be fixed to the beautiful

Tu sais que nos rapports ne sont pas tout à fait au beau fixe en ce moment.

You know our relations are a bit strained at the moment.

ⓘ *Au beau fixe* is a meteorological term meaning 'set to fair' as on a barometer.

- ***nous sommes en froid*** – things are a bit strained between us

Literally: we are in cold

Ne lui parle pas de son compagnon ; elle est en froid avec lui en ce moment.

Don't talk to her about her partner; things are a bit strained between them at the moment.

- ***poser un lapin à quelqu'un**** – to stand somebody up

Literally: to put down a rabbit to somebody

« *Tu as vu Sami hier soir ?
– Non, je l'ai attendu comme prévu devant le cinéma mais il m'a posé un lapin.* »

'Did you see Sami last night?'
'No, I waited for him in front of the cinema as we'd arranged but he stood me up.'

According to *le Robert Dictionnaire historique de la langue française*, this expression dates back to the 18th century when a coach driver would squeeze an extra person into his coach and this traveller would be called *un lapin*. Think of an overcrowded rabbit hutch.

In the 19th century the rabbit, *le lapin,* became the extra passenger whose fare was pocketed by the conductor, so its meaning became associated with something underhand.

The slang expression *poser un lapin* then came to mean 'having sex with a prostitute without paying for it'. It generally became associated with the idea of letting someone down, and finally by 1881, with the idea of not turning up for a date.

- ***regarder quelqu'un avec des yeux de merlan frit*** – to look at somebody like a lovesick puppy; to stare at somebody in astonishment or stupefaction

Literally: to look at somebody with eyes of fried whiting

Il avait le béguin pour sa prof d'espagnol, et il la regardait avec des yeux de merlan frit pendant tout le cours.

He had a crush on his Spanish teacher, and he was looking at her like a lovesick puppy the whole lesson through.

A fish in a frying pan has its mouth gaping wide open and its eyes bulging – the exaggerated expression of someone looking lovesick.

- ***se prendre un râteau par quelqu'un*** * – to be blown out by somebody; to have one's advances rejected by somebody

Literally: to take a rake to oneself by somebody

Tu veux inviter la belle Isabelle à sortir avec toi ? Vas-y mais tu risques de te prendre un râteau.

You want to ask the beautiful Isabelle to go out with you? Go ahead but you risk being rejected.

Being rejected could well feel like being hit in the face by a rake when you inadvertently step on the end of it, like in the gags of silent movies.

The opposite of being rejected might be to give a French kiss, *rouler une pelle à quelqu'un,* 'to roll a shovel to somebody', so maybe the two gardening expressions evolved as opposites of each other!

Of course, the verb *rater* meaning 'to fail' sounds rather like *râteau*, and this would no doubt have helped the expression embed itself in the language.

- ***trouver chaussure à son pied*** – to find a good match; to find what one needs

Literally: to find shoe to your foot

C'est à désespérer ! J'ai trente-cinq ans. Je ne trouverai jamais chaussure à mon pied !

Sometimes I despair! I'm thirty-five. I'll never find the right person for me!

As feet vary in length, width, lumps and bumps, it can be difficult to find exactly the right shape and size of shoe to bring us happiness and comfort. Finding a life partner is also difficult, but when we have found exactly the right soul mate, we can feel at ease, and maybe, just like Cinderella, we will live happily ever after!

The version of Cinderella most widely known in France is that written in 1697 by Charles Perrault called *Cendrillon ou la petite pantoufle de verre* – 'Cinderella or the little glass slipper'. Psychoanalysts have in the past had a field-day considering the significance of the glass slipper and the foot in the tale of Cinderella. According to Bruno Bettelheim (the now largely discredited 20th century psychoanalyst) and others, it was not by chance that Perrault chose a glass slipper into which a part of the body might slide and be held tightly, as the glass slipper symbolised the vagina, and the foot, the penis. The fact that glass might break if forced would represent the breaking of the hymen, and something which is lost at the end of a ball might well be virginity. And all this might be nonsense and it is just a simple fairy tale!

- ***un(e) de perdu(e), dix de retrouvé(e)s (proverbe)*** – there are plenty more fish in the sea (proverb)

Literally: one lost, ten found

Tu sais ce qu'il m'a dit, mon abruti de frère, quand ma fiancée m'a quitté ? « T'inquiète pas, Michel, une de perdue, dix de retrouvées ! »

Do you know what my jackass of a brother said to me when my fiancée left me? 'Don't worry! There are plenty more fish in the sea!'

ⓘ You can use this proverb to say that anything of value can be easily replaced, be it an object or a person, but it is most often used to try to console someone when a romantic relationship ends.

Quiz 10

1. *Je ne suis pas ton copain. Je suis ton professeur. On n'a pas élevé ... ensemble.*
a) *les enfants*
b) *les lions*
c) *les cochons*

2. *Je suis tombé amoureux de Sylvie. J'ai eu le coup de ... pour elle.*
a) *barre*
b) *foudre*
c) *cafard*

3. *Jules ne peut plus partir en vacances avec ses copains parce qu'il a un fil ...*
a) *à la pâtée.*
b) *au pâté.*
c) *à la patte.*

4. *« Ils se connaissent ?*
– Oui, ils sont copains comme ... »
a) *cochons.*
b) *moutons.*
c) *vaches.*

5. *Quand tu tombes amoureux/amoureuse de quelqu'un, tu as... pour lui/elle.*
a) *le bonnet*
b) *le bob*
c) *le béguin*

6. *Nos rapports ne sont pas ...*
a) *à l'orage fixe.*
b) *à la beau fixe.*
c) *au beau fixe.*

7. *Tu voudrais trouver ... ? Bienvenue sur notre site de rencontre !*
a) *chaussures à tes pieds*
b) *pantoufles à tes pieds*
c) *chaussure à ton pied*

8. *Demain c'est l'anniversaire de maman. Papa va être aux ... soins pour elle.*
a) *grands*
b) *petits*
c) *gros*

9. *Arrête de la regarder avec des yeux de ... frit !*
a) *morue*
b) *merlan*
c) *saumon*

10. *Depuis le jour où il est rentré de Thaïlande tatoué du prénom « Suzie », Mélanie, sa femme, est ... avec lui.*
a) *en froid*
b) *en chaud*
c) *en hiver*

11. *Elle est... dingue de moi.*
a) *raide*
b) *bleu*
c) *rose*

12. « Les deux garçons s'entendent bien ?
– Oui, ils sont comme cul et ... »
a) veste.
b) chemise.
c) slip.

13. Il lui dit qu'il va quitter sa femme pour elle, et Martine le croit, la pauvre idiote ! L'amour rend ..., n'est-ce pas !
a) aveugle
b) imbécile
c) stupide

14. Ce matin Romain m'a dit qu'il est tombé amoureux de Mathilde. Il y a deux semaines, c'était Lola. Il a un cœur d' ... !
a) ananas
b) avocat
c) artichaut

15. Quand Sacha m'a quittée, maman m'a dit : « ... »
a) Un de perdu, dix de retrouvés.
b) Un de perdu, deux de trouvés.
c) Un de retrouvé, dix de perdus.

16. J'ai invité Hélène à sortir avec moi samedi, mais je me suis pris ...
a) une brosse.
b) une bêche.
c) un râteau.

17. J'ai attendu Jordane pendant une heure, mais elle n'est pas venue. Elle m'a posé …
a) un lièvre.
b) un lapin.
c) un Lapon.

18. C'est un vrai don Juan, un … des cœurs.
a) bureau
b) bourreau
c) éboueur

19. Deux semaines avant le mariage, Timéo est parti avec ses copains pour … sa vie de garçon.
a) enterrer
b) déterrer
c) entêter

20. J'ai trouvé une marguerite et j'ai arraché un à un les pétales en disant : « M'aime-t-il ? … »
a) un peu, passionnément, beaucoup, pas du tout, à la folie !
b) un peu, passionnément, à la folie, pas du tout, beaucoup !
c) un peu, beaucoup, passionnément, à la folie, pas du tout !

Answers 10

1.	c	11.	a
2.	b	12.	b
3.	c	13.	a
4.	a	14.	c
5.	c	15.	a
6.	c	16.	c
7.	c	17.	b
8.	b	18.	b
9.	b	19.	a
10.	a	20.	c

Afterword

Had this been a work of fiction, my editor would no doubt have been exhorting me not to use clichés! Learning these 200 well known and loved expressions will not make your thoughts sound fresh and original, but I hope they will enable you to fit in better with French society and help you to form cross-cultural friendships which will last a lifetime. *Quel bonheur !*

Remember, not every French person knows every French expression, so do not be surprised if your French friends don't know all 200 of these expressions! There might also be some debate as to which version is the one in most frequent use. In writing this text, I have often swung from one version to another as my French friends have argued the point between them. It's all part of the fun, though!

If you have enjoyed this book, please do tell people and leave a review on Amazon. If you have any questions or suggestions, please contact me directly at clare@figureoutfrench.com.

Amitiés !

Clare

Complete List of Expressions

CHAPTER 1

Manger et boire – eating and drinking

avoir ou *crever la dalle*** – to be starving hungry

avoir l'estomac dans les talons – to be famished *or* starving

avoir les crocs – to be famished *or* starving

avoir un bon coup de fourchette – to have a hearty appetite

avoir un petit creux – to feel a little hungry

avoir une faim de loup – to be as hungry as a wolf

boire à sa soif ; manger à sa faim – to satisfy one's thirst; to eat one's fill

Bon appétit ! – enjoy your meal!

c'est du jus de chaussette – it's like dishwater

c'est mon péché mignon – it's my guilty pleasure; it's my (little) weakness; I have a weakness for it

*ce n'est pas de refus** – I wouldn't say no

croquer ou *dévorer* ou *mordre quelque chose à belles dents* – to wolf something down

*déjeuner sur le pouce** – to have a quick snack

*dîner à la bonne franquette** – to have an informal *or* pot luck dinner

entre la poire et le fromage – during a quiet, relaxed moment between two events *faire la fine bouche* – to be picky; to turn one's nose up at things which are generally appreciated

je n'en peux plus – I'm full

l'appétit vient en mangeant (proverbe) – eating whets the appetite; (figuratively) the more you have, the more you want

manger comme quatre – to eat like a horse

manger ou *dévorer comme un ogre* – to eat like a horse

CHAPTER 2

Manger et boire (suite) – eating and drinking (cont.)

manger du bout des dents – to pick at one's food

mettre les petits plats dans les grands – to lay on a first-rate meal; to go to great effort or expense to please somebody

mieux vaut l'avoir en photo qu'à (sa) table ou *qu'en vacances* ou *qu'en pension* – he'll *or* she'll eat you (/us, etc.) out of house and home

la note est salée* – the bill is a bit steep

qui dort dîne (proverbe) – he who sleeps forgets his hunger

s'en mettre ou *s'en fourrer jusque là** – to stuff oneself*; to feed one's face*; to have a slap-up meal*; to have a real blow out*; to have a nosh-up* (UK)

tenir table ouverte – to keep open house

vous m'en direz des nouvelles – you will like it

L'alcool – alcohol

À la tienne Étienne !* – Cheers!*

avoir la gueule de bois* – to have a hangover

avoir le vin mauvais ou *gai* ou *triste* – to get nasty or happy or sad after a few drinks

avoir un (p'tit) coup dans le nez* – to have had one too many or a drop too much; to be in a very bad way

avoir un verre dans le nez* – to have had one too many or a bit too much to drink

avoir une bonne descente* – to be able to really knock it back*

boire cul sec – to drink down in one

ça s'arrose !* – let's drink to that; that calls for a drink

être beurré(e) (comme un p'tit Lu)** – to be sloshed* or plastered*

être soûl(e) comme un cochon – to be as drunk as a Lord

soûl comme un Polonais – as drunk as a Lord

il/elle boit comme un trou – he/she drinks like a fish

il/elle est ivre mort – he/she is blind drunk

il/elle est plein(e) comme une barrique* – he/she is completely drunk

être rond comme une queue de pelle* – to be rolling drunk

prendre une cuite** – to get plastered*; to get sloshed*

se mettre au régime sec – to go on the wagon; to stop drinking alcohol

CHAPTER 3

Apprécier la vie – enjoying life

à tire-larigot* – to your heart's content; like there's no tomorrow

avoir les doigts de pied en éventail – to have one's feet up

chanter à tue-tête – to sing at the top of one's voice

chanter en yaourt* – to sing in mangled English

chanter comme une casserole* – to be a lousy* singer

Cool, Raoul !* Relax, Max !* – Chill out !*

À l'aise, Blaise ! – at ease!

Tu parles, Charles ! – you bet!

Je te le donne en mille, Émile ! – you'll never guess!

Tu l'as dit, bouffi ! – you said it!

croquer la vie à pleines dents – to make the most of life

démarrer sur les chapeaux de roues* – to get off to a fast start *or* a flying start

être à la fête – to be having a field day; to be one's day

être tout feu tout flamme – to be wildly enthusiastic; to be full of enthusiasm

faire la fête à quelqu'un – to give somebody a warm welcome *or* reception *faire sa fête à quelqu'un*** – to beat somebody up

faire le lézard* ; *lézarder** *au soleil* – to bask in the sun

faire les quatre cents coups – to paint the town red; to raise merry hell

faire un tabac* – to be a hit

marcher (comme) sur des roulettes* – to go like clockwork; to go (off) very smoothly

Minute papillon ! – Just a minute! *or* Hold your horses! *or* Not so fast!

Quand on parle du loup (on en voit la queue) (proverbe) – Speak of the devil (and he's sure to appear) (proverb)

s'en donner à cœur joie – to have a tremendous time; to go to town

trouver son bonheur – to find what one is looking for *or* what one wants

voir la vie en rose – to see everything through rose-coloured spectacles

CHAPTER 4

Les rires – laughter

c'était à mourir de rire – it would make you die laughing; it was hysterical*

c'était à se rouler par terre* – it would make you die laughing; it was hysterical*; rolling on the ground *or* floor laughing*

à se taper le cul par terre*** - it was hysterical*

être plié (en deux ou en quatre); être plié de rire – to be doubled up with laughter

plus on est de fous, plus on rit ! – the more the merrier!

rira bien qui rira le dernier (proverbe) – he who laughs last laughs longest (proverb)

rire à gorge déployée – to scream *or* roar with laughter

rire jaune – to give a forced laugh

se fendre la poire** ou la gueule** ou la pipe** ou la pêche** – to laugh one's head off *or* to split one's sides laughing

une plaisanterie qui vole bas – a feeble joke; a joke in poor taste

Le bonheur – happiness

avoir le moral ; avoir (un) bon moral ; avoir un moral d'acier – to be in good spirits; to have a high morale

être aux anges – to be in heaven; to be over the moon*

je me sentais pousser des ailes – I was walking *or* treading on air; I felt as if I'd grown wings

tout baigne (dans l'huile)* ; ça baigne * – everything's hunky-dory

La bonne santé – good health

avoir bon pied bon œil – to be fit as a fiddle

avoir de l'énergie à revendre – to have energy to spare *or* galore *or* in spades*

avoir la frite* ou la patate* – to feel great; to be in great shape; to have lots of energy

donner la frite à quelqu'un – to cheer somebody up

garder la frite – to still feel good

avoir la pêche* – to be on form; to be in high spirits; to have lots of energy; to be feeling peachy*

péter le feu** – to be full of energy; to be full of beans (UK)

reprendre du poil de la bête* – to regain strength; to pick up again

se remettre sur pied – to get back on one's feet

CHAPTER 5

La négativité – negativity

avoir droit à ou *manger la soupe à la grimace* – to get a frosty reception; to be in the dog house

ça ne casse pas trois pattes à un canard* – it's nothing to write home about; it's nothing to get excited about

ça ne mange pas de pain – it doesn't cost anything; it can't hurt

en voir des vertes et des pas mûres* – to go through a lot; to experience some hard knocks; to go through the mill

il en a dit des vertes (et des pas mûres)* – he came out with some pretty risqué stuff*

j'en ai entendu des vertes et des pas mûres sur son compte !* – you wouldn't believe the things I've heard about him!

Est-ce que je te demande si ta grand-mère fait du vélo ? – Who asked you for your opinion?; Who asked you to put in your two pennies' worth? * (UK)

Et ta sœur ? – Who asked you for your opinion?; Who asked you to put in your two pennies' worth? * (UK)

être ou *rester le bec dans l'eau** – to be left in the lurch *or* to be left high and dry *or* to be let down

*clouer le bec à quelqu'un** – to reduce somebody to silence; to shut somebody up

défendre quelque chose bec et ongles – to fight tooth and nail for something

*faire tourner quelqu'un en bourrique** – to drive somebody to distraction; to drive somebody up the wall

(il ne) faut pas pousser le bouchon trop loin – that's pushing it too far

il ne faut pas pousser mémé ou *mémère* ou *grand-mère dans les orties** ou *dans les bégonias** – that's pushing it too far; let's not get carried away; you must not be antisocial

(il ne) manquait plus que ça ! – that's the last thing I (*or* you, etc.) needed!; that's all I (*or* you, etc.) needed!

il y a anguille sous roche – something is hidden; something is afoot; something fishy is going on

il n'y a pas de quoi pavoiser ! – it's nothing to get excited about *or* to write home about!

jamais deux sans trois – good *or* bad things come in threes; three is the magic number

je n'y suis pour rien – I have nothing to do with it; it's nothing to do with me *mon sang n'a fait qu'un tour* – I saw red; it made my blood boil; it made my blood run cold

ne pas en mener large ; n'en mener pas large – to have one's heart in one's boots; to be feeling worried and lacking in confidence ; to be in a difficult *or* embarrassing situation and to let this show; to feel intimidated

partir en cacahuète* ou cacahouète* – to go to the dogs*; to go downhill

se plaindre pour un pet de travers** – to be always complaining about one's health

Les maladies et la physiologie – illnesses and physiology

à vos souhaits !* / à tes souhaits !* – bless you!

À tes/vos amours ! – to your loves!

Et que les tiennes/les vôtres durent toujours ! – and may yours last forever!

avoir la chair de poule – to have goose bumps *or* goose pimples

CHAPTER 6

Les maladies et la physiologie (suite) – illnesses and physiology (cont.)

avoir les jambes en coton* ou en flanelle* – to have legs like jelly

avoir les nerfs à fleur de peau – to be over-sensitive *or* irritable; to be all on edge *être à bout de nerfs* – to be all on edge

avoir les nerfs à vif – to be all on edge

avoir les nerfs en boule – to be all on edge

avoir les nerfs en pelote – to be all on edge

c'est une vraie boule/pelote de nerfs – he/she is a real ball of nerves

avoir mal au cœur – to feel sick

avoir un haut-le-cœur – to retch *or* to gag

Haut les cœurs ! – lift up your spirits! take heart! be brave! have courage!

avoir un chat dans la gorge – to have a frog in the throat

avoir un cheveu sur la langue – to lisp

avoir un coup de barre* – to feel drained *or* shattered quite suddenly

c'est le coup de barre* dans ce restaurant – you pay through the nose in this restaurant

avoir un coup de mou* – to suddenly feel weak, limp *or* lethargic; to slacken off

avoir un coup de pompe* – to feel drained *or* shattered quite suddenly

avoir un (petit) grain (de folie)* – to have a touch of madness; to be a bit touched

avoir une case (de) vide* ; avoir une case en moins* – to have a screw loose *il lui manque une case** – he's got a screw loose

être à l'ouest* – to be out of it* *or* not with it*; to be unable to concentrate; to have one's head in the clouds

être dans tous ses états – to be in a terrible state; to be in a state of extreme agitation

être myope comme une taupe – to be as blind as a bat

être sur les rotules* – to be exhausted; to be on one's knees with fatigue

être sur les genoux – to be on one's knees

être à genoux (devant quelqu'un) – to be on one's knees (before someone) i.e. to kneel in submission.

faire un mal de chien* – to really hurt

avoir un mal de chien – to have great difficulty

filer un mauvais coton* – (physically) to be very low; to be in a bad way; to be wasting away; (morally) to be getting into bad ways

c'est coton – it's difficult

je ne suis pas dans mon assiette* – I'm not feeling quite myself; I'm feeling a bit off-colour

je suis à côté de mes pompes* – I'm not quite with it; I'm really out of it

marcher à côté de ses pompes* – to be not quite with it; to have one's head in the clouds

je suis ou *je me sens mal dans ma peau* – I'm ill at ease with myself; I don't feel comfortable in my body; things aren't right with me

être à l'aise ou *bien dans ses pompes* – to feel good

CHAPTER 7

Les maladies et la physiologie (suite) – illnesses and physiology (cont.)

ne pas avoir les yeux en face des trous* – to not see clearly what is in front of you; to be not with it*; to be half asleep; to be too tired to think straight

passer sur le billard* – to have an operation

perdre les pédales* – to get all mixed up; to lose one's head *or* marbles*

perdre la boule* – to go bonkers* *or* nuts*; to go off one's rocker*

mieux vaut prévenir que guérir (proverbe) – prevention is better than cure (proverb)

se mélanger les pieds* ou *les pédales** ou *les pinceaux** ou *les crayons** – to get into a muddle

sucrer les fraises** – to have a nervous tremble; to become senile

tomber dans les pommes* – to faint; to pass out

rester dans les pommes* – to stay out cold; to remain unconscious

tourner de l'œil – to faint; to pass out; to keel over

Le sommeil – sleep

dormir ou *coucher à la belle étoile* – to sleep under the stars *dormir à poings fermés* – to sleep like a log

dormir comme un loir ou *une marmotte* ou *une souche* ou *une bûche* – to sleep like a log

dormir sur ses deux oreilles – to sleep soundly; to sleep safely (in one's bed)

faire la grasse matinée – to have a lie in

passer une nuit blanche – to have a sleepless night

piquer du nez dans ou *sur son assiette** – to nod off (during a meal); to hang one's head in shame

s'endormir comme une masse – to go out like a light; to fall asleep quickly

La mort – death

avoir un pied dans la tombe – to have one foot in the grave

ça sent le sapin* – the end is near; he *or* she has one foot in the grave

casser sa pipe* – to kick the bucket**; to snuff it**

faire le grand saut – to meet one's final hour

CHAPTER 8

La mort (suite) – death (cont.)

manger les pissenlits par la racine* – to be pushing up daisies*; to be dead and buried

mourir de sa belle mort – to die a natural death

passer l'arme à gauche* – to kick the bucket**

rendre l'âme – to give up the ghost

tomber raide mort – to drop down dead

La chance – luck

avoir du pot* ou *du bol** – to be lucky

avoir du cul*** – to be lucky

avoir le cul*** bordé de nouilles – to be very lucky

c'est au petit bonheur (la chance) – it's just the luck of the draw; it's pot luck ; it's haphazard

c'est la faute à pas de chance – it's just bad luck

Le sport – sport

faire cavalier seul – to go it alone

faire mouche – to hit the bull's-eye; to score a bull's-eye; (figuratively) to score; to hit home; to hit a sensitive point

gagner ou *arriver dans un fauteuil** – to romp home; to win easily

gagner haut la main – to win hands down

gagner les doigts dans le nez* – to win easily *or* hands down

mettre ou *taper (en plein) dans le mille** – to hit a bull's-eye; to be bang on target*; to hit the nail on the head

mettre quelqu'un KO* – to knock somebody out *or* for six *nager comme un fer à repasser** – to swim like a brick

saisir la balle au bond – to seize the opportunity (while the going is good); to be sharp-witted in discussion

se mettre en jambe(s)* – to warm up

tirer ou *retirer son épingle du jeu* – to play one's game well; to extricate oneself (without losing money)

se tirer d'affaire – to pull through; to get out of a tight spot

être en jeu – to be at stake

mettre tout en jeu – to risk everything

y a pas photo* – there's no question about it; there's no competition; there's a big difference

CHAPTER 9

L'attirance et l'apparence – attraction and appearance

à poil** – stark naked

avoir ou *faire une partie de jambes en l'air*** – to have a roll in the hay*; to have some hanky-panky*; to bonk**

avoir un œil qui dit merde*** à l'autre – to squint; to be cross-eyed

avoir un œil qui joue au billard et l'autre qui compte les points – to squint; to be cross-eyed

bas les pattes !* – keep your hands to yourself

battre la chamade – to pound; to beat wildly

beau ou *belle à croquer* – as pretty as a picture; good enough to eat

dans le plus simple appareil (humoristique) – in one's birthday suit (humorous) *or* in the altogether; naked *or* very nearly naked

elle lui a tapé dans l'œil* – he fancied her*; she piqued his interest; she caught his eye

en tout bien tout honneur – above board; in all innocence

envoyer un baiser de la main – to blow a kiss

habillé(e) ou *ficelé(e)* ou *fagoté(e) comme l'as de pique** – dressed any old how

joli(e) comme un cœur – as pretty as a picture

maigre comme un clou – as thin as a rake

maquillé(e) comme un camion volé* ou *une voiture volée** – wearing an excessive amount of makeup

on dirait qu'elle ou *qu'il a un pot de peinture sur le visage* ou *la tête* – she *or* he is wearing far too much makeup

c'est un vrai pot de peinture – she *or* he is wearing far too much makeup

moche comme un pou* – as ugly as sin; a face like the back of a bus

nu(e) comme un ver – stark naked

rouler un patin** ou *une pelle** à quelqu'un* – to give somebody a French kiss

se coiffer avec un pétard* – to have scruffy hair

se mettre sur son trente et un* – to be dressed to kill; to get dressed up to the nines; to dress one's best

tiré à quatre épingles – dressed up to the nines; (too) smartly dressed

CHAPTER 10

L'amour, le mariage et l'amitié – love, marriage and friendship

l'amour rend aveugle ; l'amour est aveugle (proverbe) – love is blind (proverb)

avoir élevé ou *gardé les cochons ensemble** – to have been close since childhood; to be old pals

avoir le béguin pour quelqu'un* – to have a crush on somebody

(*se*) *toquer de quelqu'un / quelque chose* – to go crazy over somebody *or* something

avoir le coup de foudre pour quelqu'un – to fall head over heels in love with somebody

ce fut le coup de foudre – it was love at first sight

avoir ou *être un cœur d'artichaut* – to be soft-hearted and fall in love easily

avoir un fil à la patte* – to be tied down

un bourreau des cœurs – a lady-killer *or* a heart-breaker; a fast worker

enterrer sa vie de garçon – to have a stag party

enterrer sa vie de jeune fille – to have a hen party

enterrer sa vie de célibataire – to have a stag or hen party

être aux petits soins pour quelqu'un – to dance attendance on somebody; to wait on somebody hand and foot

*être comme cul et chemise avec quelqu'un** – to be as thick as thieves with somebody

*être copains comme cochons** – to be great buddies

*être raide dingue de quelqu'un** – to be completely crazy about somebody

M'aime-t-il ou *M'aime-t-elle ? Un peu, beaucoup, passionnément, à la folie, pas du tout* – He loves me, he loves me not; she loves me, she loves me not.

ne pas être au beau fixe – (relationships) to be a bit strained

nous sommes en froid – things are a bit strained between us

*poser un lapin à quelqu'un** – to stand somebody up

regarder quelqu'un avec des yeux de merlan frit – to look at somebody like a lovesick puppy; to stare at somebody in astonishment or stupefaction

*se prendre un râteau par quelqu'un** – to be blown out by somebody; to have one's advances rejected by somebody

trouver chaussure à son pied – to find a good match; to find what one needs

un(e) de perdu(e), dix de retrouvé(e)s (proverbe) – there are plenty more fish in the sea (proverb)

More about the Author

Clare Jones was lucky enough to have excellent teachers at Notre Dame High School, St Helens, who gave her a love of the French language. When her hometown arranged a cultural exchange with Chalon sur Saône in Burgundy, she was extremely fortunate to be placed with a family who gave her a lasting appreciation of French culture, and friendships which have spanned three generations. She went on to study French at Leicester University and after her degree, she trained as a teacher. Her first book was self-published in 2015 – *Je mourrai moins bête: 200 French expressions to help you die less stupid*.

Clare is now very busy working as a French tutor in Oundle, Northamptonshire, and she has students across the world thanks to the magic of the internet. She is happy to be contacted.

Send her an email at **clare@figureoutfrench.com.**

For lessons on Zoom, visit her tuition website at **www.frenchtuition-northants.co.uk.**

Like her page on Facebook: **FigureOutFrench**

Follow her on Twitter: **@FigureOutFrench**

Read her blog at **www.figureoutfrench.com**.

More about the Illustrator

Tamsin Edwards studied art at Nene Art College, Northampton and Derby School of Art during the early 1980s.

Though well known for her atmospheric landscapes, she also enjoys creating quirky pen & wash illustrations, often portraying comic images of people and places.

Tamsin has previously collaborated with Clare Jones to produce an iPhone application, in addition to the French language book *Je mourrai moins bête: 200 French expressions to help you die less stupid*. Other past commissioned projects include illustrating the children's storybook *Tales of Two Shires*, a book of poetic verse and a satirical publication of Greek mythology.

As well as regularly exhibiting artwork and selling to clients around the world, Tamsin has also had several of her works published in an international art magazine.

To view further examples of her work, please visit www.texart.co.uk.

Tamsin can be contacted at art@texart.co.uk.

By the same author and illustrator

Je mourrai moins bête: 200 French expressions to help you die less stupid

ISBN-10:1519107684

ISBN-13:978-1519107688

Printed by CreateSpace, An Amazon.com Company, 2015

'With more than 200 expressions covering a wide range of areas and wonderful illustrations, "Je mourrai moins bête" is a great way to learn more about the quirky French way of seeing the world. You will get the expression, the equivalent in English, an explanation of its origin and to top it all, regular quizzes to test your knowledge! Perfect! Written in a witty and very engaging way, this book will make you laugh and learn at the same time. Students of French will love it and French students of English will also find the translations very useful. After all, you don't want to be stared at when you gleefully talk about "making the bridge" during a bank holiday weekend or "to be in the cabbages" when you are sad after failing something, do you??' Ariane Bogain, Senior Lecturer in Languages, Northumbria University

'I must say, I just love this little book and enjoy very much your cheerful spirit of inquiry and your generosity in sharing this amazing accumulation of information!' Timothy L. Wilkerson, Associate Professor of Languages, Wittenberg University, Ohio

Bibliography

BERNET, Charles and RÉZEAU, Pierre, *On va le dire comme ça, Dictionnaire des expressions quotidiennes*, Paris : Balland, 2008

BORTON, Arnold and MAUFFRAIS, Henri, *Learn to Speak Like the French, French Idiomatic Expressions*, Durham: Eloquent Books, 2010

CARADEC, François and POUY Jean-Bernard, *Dictionnaire du français argotique et populaire*, Paris: Larousse, 2009

COLLINS, Lauren, *When in French, Love in a second language*, HarperCollins Publishers, London, 2017

Collins Robert French dictionary, HarperCollins Publishers, Glasgow, 2006

DUNETON, Claude, *La Puce à l'oreille, Anthologie des expressions populaires avec leur origine*, Le Livre de Poche, 1990

GRANEK, Esther, *Portraits et chansons sans retouches*, éditions saint-germain-des-prés,1976

GUIRAUD, Pierre, *Les Locutions françaises*, Presses Universitaires de France, 1973

LEVY, Marc, *La prochaine fois,* © Éditions Robert Laffont, 2004

REY, Alain, *Le Dictionnaire historique de la langue française*, Paris: Dictionnaires Le Robert, 2006

VERGER, Gregory, L'Express/L'Impartial, *A l'école des bonnes manières, « bon appétit » est banni !* 11.9.10

WERTENBAKER, Timberlake, translation of Racine's '*Britannicus*', Faber & Faber, October 2011

Websites

All URLs were collected in May 2019

unless otherwise stated.

A la tienne, le webzine des amateurs d'alcool, *'Origine de l'expression « à la tienne »'*, https://alatienne.fr/definition-a-la-tienne/

About-France.com,

- 'The French healthcare system', https://about-france.com/health-care.htm

- 'Getting medical help in France', https://about-france.com/medical-help.htm

Académie française, *'humeur, humour'* Le 10 juillet 2012, http://www.academie-francaise.fr/humeur-humour

bmlisieux.com, JOLIMONT, Théodore de (1787-18.) : *'De l'usage de saluer et d'adresser des souhaits à ceux qui éternuent'*, http://www.bmlisieux.com/curiosa/delusage.htm

Cambridge Dictionary, https://dictionary.cambridge.org/dictionary/french-english/

Centre National de Ressources Textuelles et Lexicales, https://www.cnrtl.fr/

Chansons à boire, https://tinyurl.com/y43ftx9d

Culture Presse, Union des commerçants des loisirs et de la presse, *'Les Jeux (FDJ et PMU)'*, https://tinyurl.com/yyxglt42

L'ekchprechion du zour, 'des vertes et des pas mûres', https://tinyurl.com/y2esxnzk

Eurostat,

- 'Healthy life years and life expectancy at birth, by sex', https://tinyurl.com/y547o6wr

- 'Hospital beds', https://tinyurl.com/yyrd5fko

Expressio.fr, Georges Planelles, the best online resource there is, http://www.expressio.fr/index.php

Le Figaro, *'Bac de Philo : les corrigés des sujets de la section STG en vidéo'*, https://tinyurl.com/y47qxd6h

france24.com, "'Le binge drinking' on the rise in France", https://tinyurl.com/yyc6rerz

France Culture podcast, *'Privatisation de la Française des jeux : un pari risqué ?'*, https://tinyurl.com/yxcx5844

French Moments Blog, *'Quelques mots sur l'humour français'* Publié le 25 août 2012 par French Moments, https://tinyurl.com/y3ulbf7z

Harris Interactive, 'THEME 3 : « LES FRANÇAIS ET LEUR RAPPORT AU SPORT »', https://tinyurl.com/y4e44y86

languefrancaise.net/Bob, *'soûl comme un cochon'*, www.languefrancaise.net/Bob/31510

lintern@ute, https://www.linternaute.com/

TheLocal.fr, "*Is it true 'the French just can't laugh at themselves'?*", https://tinyurl.com/y5e66tqj

Le Monde, *'Bacs S, ES et L 2015 : découvrez les sujets de philo'*, https://tinyurl.com/y5kvxqg7

OECD, 'Balancing paid work, unpaid work and leisure', https://tinyurl.com/ydb9jvr9

Le Parisien, *'Bac 2015 : découvrez les sujets de l'épreuve de philosophie'*, https://tinyurl.com/yxo237cp

Revue Lorraine Populaire, *jus de chaussette (collected 2013 – no longer live link)*

Tennis fédération française, Comité Français de Courte-Paume: *saisir la balle au bond*, http://goo.gl/KTLT6

Thoughtco, 'Avoir la frite', https://www.thoughtco.com/avoir-la-frite-1371103

Le Trésor de la langue française informatisé, ("le TLFi"), http://atilf.atilf.fr/

Wikipédia,

- 'les quatre cents coups', https://tinyurl.com/y48yg6dy
- 'sieste', https://tinyurl.com/y3h3nrkc
- *'Le Dormeur du val'*, https://tinyurl.com/y3tx9v6r
- *'Demain dès l'aube'*, https://tinyurl.com/y2zp7cbu
- *'Cendrillon ou la Petite Pantoufle de verre'*, https://tinyurl.com/cgqpgp7

WordReference.com Language forums, https://www.wordreference.com/

YouTube, *'Tu pousses le bouchon un peu trop loin, Maurice !'* https://tinyurl.com/odzywec

INDEX

A

Académie française l', 37
affaire, se tirer d', 149,
ailes, je me sentais pousser des, 68
aise, Blaise !, À l' 48
alcohol, 30-39
âme, rendre l', 140
amour rend aveugle l', 175
amours !, À tes, 94
anges, être aux, 67
anguille sous roche, il y a, 88
appareil, dans le plus simple, 160
appétit !, Bon, 13
appétit vient en mangeant, l', 18-19
arme à gauche, passer l', 139
arrose !, ça s', 34
as de pique, habillé(e) ou ficelé(e) ou fagoté(e) comme l', 163
assiette, je ne suis pas dans mon, 111
Astérix, 61
attraction and appearance, 156-169

B

baccalauréat, 9
baigne, ça, 68,69
baiser de la main, envoyer un, 162
balle au bond, saisir la, 147
banane, avoir la, 72
barrique, plein(e) comme une, 38
beau fixe, ne pas être au, 184
beau ou belle à croquer, 159
bec à quelqu'un, clouer le 85
bec dans l'eau, être ou rester le, 85
bec et ongles, défendre quelque chose 85
bégonias, 87
béguin pour quelqu'un, avoir le, 176,177
beurré(e) (comme un p'tit Lu), être, 35
Bible, 95
billard, passer sur le, 120
bol, avoir du, 141
bonheur (la chance), c'est au petit, 142
bonheur, trouver son, 55
bouche, faire la fine, 17
bouchon trop loin, (il ne) faut pas pousser le, 86
boule, perdre la, 121
bourreau des cœurs, un, 179
bourrique, faire tourner quelqu'un en, 86
Braille, Louis, 129
Britannicus, 161
bûche, dormir comme une, 126

C

cacahuète, partir en, 92
camion volé, maquillé(e) comme un, 164
Canard enchaîné, Le, 54,61
canard, ça ne casse pas trois pattes à un, 82
Caroline, 184
case (de) vide, avoir une, 107
casserole, chanter comme une, 47
cavalier seul, faire, 143
chair de poule, avoir la, 95
chamade, battre la, 159

chapeaux de roues, démarrer sur les, 49
Charlie Hebdo, 61
chat dans la gorge, avoir un, 103
chaussure à son pied, trouver, 188
cheveu sur la langue, avoir un, 104
Clarke, Stephen, 61
clou, maigre comme un, 164
cochon, être copains comme, 182
cochon, être soûl(e) comme un, 36
cochons ensemble, avoir élevé ou gardé les, 176
cœur d'artichaut, avoir ou être un, 178
cœur joie, s'en donner à, 54
cœur volcan, Le, 159
Coloris, 156
Cool, Raoul ! Relax, Max !, 48
copains comme cochons, être, 182
Corneille, 161
coton, c'est, 111
coton, filer un mauvais, 110
coup dans le nez, avoir un (p'tit), 33
coup de barre, avoir un, 104, 105
coup de foudre pour quelqu'un, avoir le, 178
coup de pompe, avoir un, 106
crayons, se mélanger les, 122
creux, avoir un petit, 11
crocs, avoir les, 10
cuite, prendre une, 39
cul, avoir du, 142
cul bordé de nouilles, avoir le, 142
cul et chemise avec quelqu'un, être comme, 181
cul par terre, à se taper le, 62
cul sec, boire, 34

Curie, Pierre and Marie, 129

D

dalle, avoir ou crever la, 9
death, 129-131, 137-140
Demain, dès l'aube, 137
dents, croquer la vie à pleines, 49
dents, croquer ou dévorer ou mordre quelque chose à belles, 14
dents, manger du bout des, 26
descente, avoir une bonne, 34
deux sans trois, jamais, 90
Dîner de cons, Le, 61
doigts dans le nez, gagner les, 145
doigts de pied en éventail, avoir les, 46
dormeur du Val, Le, 137
Dumas, Alexandre, 129
Duneton, Claude, 7

E

eating and drinking, 9-20, 26-30
Elmaleh, Gad, 63
emergency, medical, 93
énergie à revendre, avoir de l', 70
enjoying life, 45-55
épingle du jeu, tirer ou retirer son, 148-149
épingles, tiré à quatre, 169
estomac dans les talons, avoir l', 10
états, être dans tous ses, 108
étoile, dormir ou coucher à la belle, 125
European Commission, 101
Eurostat, 101
éventail, avoir les doigts de pied en, 46
Expressio, 106, 123, 139, 149

F

faim de loup, avoir une, 11
faim, manger à sa, 12
fast foods, les, 26
faute à pas de chance, c'est la, 142
fauteuil, gagner ou arriver dans un, 144
fer à repasser, nager comme un, 147
fête à quelqu'un, faire sa, 51
fête à quelqu'un, faire la, 50
fête, être à la, 50
feu, péter le, 72
feu tout flamme, être tout, 50
fil à la patte, avoir un, 178
flanelle, avoir les jambes en, 101
fleur de peau, avoir les nerfs à, 101
fourchette, avoir un bon coup de, 11
fous, plus on rit !, plus on est de 63
fraises, sucrer les, 122-123
franquette, dîner à la bonne, 16
frite, avoir la, 70-71
froid, nous sommes en, 185

G

Gargantua, 19
genoux, être à, 109
genoux, être sur les, 109
gorge déployée, rire à, 64
grain, avoir un (petit), 107
grand-mère fait du vélo ? Est-ce que je te demande si ta, 84
Granek, Esther, 156
gueule de bois, avoir la, 32
Guignols, Les, 61
Guiraud, Pierre, 103

H

Hallyday, Johnny, 52, 130
happiness, 66-69
Harris poll, 143
health, good, 69-73
health care, 69
honneur, en tout bien tout, 162
Hugo, Victor, 129, 137
humour, 61

I

Il pleure dans mon cœur, 80
illnesses and physiology, 93-95, 101-113, 119-125
ivre mort, il/elle est, 36

J

jambe(s), se mettre en, 148
jambes en coton, avoir les, 101
je n'en peux plus, 18
jeu, être en, 149
jeu, mettre tout en, 149
Joliment, Théodore de, 94
Juliette, 88
jus de chaussette, c'est du, 13

K

KO, mettre quelqu'un, 146

L

lapin à quelqu'un, poser un, 185
laughter, 61-66
lézard, faire le, 51
loir, dormir comme un, 126
Louiguy, 55
Louis XIII, 52
Louis-Philippe, King, 66
loup (on en voit la queue), Quand on parle du, 54

love, marriage and friendship, 175-188
luck, 141-143

M

M'aime-t-il ou M'aime-t-elle ? Un peu, beaucoup, passionnément, à la folie, pas du tout, 183
main, gagner haut la, 145
mal au cœur, avoir, 102
mal de chien, avoir un, 110
mal de chien, faire un, 110
manquait plus que ça !, (il ne), 88
Mariés au premier regard, 175
marmotte, dormir comme une, 126
masse, s'endormir comme une, 129
Mathis, Gilles, 36
matinée, faire la grasse, 127
Mc Solaar, 184
Mémé dans les orties, 88
Mémère dans les orties, 87
mener large, ne pas en 91
mettre ou s'en fourrer jusque là, s'en 29
mieux vaut prévenir que guérir, 122
mille, Émile !, Je te le donne en 48
mille, mettre ou taper (en plein) dans le, 146
mindfulness, 45
Minute papillon !, 53
Montauban, 52
moral, avoir le, 67
mort, mourir de sa belle, 139
mouche, faire, 144
mourir de rire, c'était à, 62

N

Napoleon, 36
negativity, 80-93
nerfs, 101, 102
Nestlé, 86
New Wave, French, 52
nez dans ou sur son assiette, piquer du, 129
note est salée, la, 28
nouvelles, vous m'en direz des, 30
nuit blanche, passer une, 128

O

OECD, 26
œil qui dit merde à l'autre, avoir un, 158
œil qui joue au billard et l'autre qui compte les points, avoir un, 158
œil, elle lui a tapé dans l', 161
œil, tourner de l', 124
ogre, manger ou dévorer comme un, 20
oreilles, dormir sur ses deux, 126
orties, il ne faut pas pousser mémé ou mémère ou grand-mère dans les, 87
ouest, être à l', 108

P

pain, ça ne mange pas de, 82
Panthéon, le, 129
paracetamol, 119
partie de jambes en l'air, avoir ou faire une, 157
patate, avoir la, 70
patin, rouler un, 166
pattes !, bas les, 158
pavoiser !, il n'y a pas de quoi, 89
peau, je suis ou je me sens mal dans ma, 112

péché mignon, c'est mon, 14
pêche, avoir la, 72
pédales, perdre les, 121
pelle, rouler une, 166, 188
pet de travers, se plaindre pour un, 92
pétard, se coiffer avec un, 167
Philipon, Charles, 66
philosophy, 9
photo qu'à (sa) table ou *qu'en vacances* ou *qu'en pension, mieux vaut l'avoir en*, 27
photo, y a pas, 150
Piaf, Édith, 55
pied bon œil, avoir bon, 69
pied dans la tombe, avoir un, 130
pied, se remettre sur, 74
pieds, se mélanger les, 122
pinceaux, se mélanger les 122
pipe, casser sa, 131
pissenlits par la racine, manger les, 138
plaisanterie qui vole bas, une, 66
Planelles, Georges, 7, 85, 123, 166, 167, 182
plié(e) (en deux ou *en quatre), être*, 63
plié(e) de rire, être, 63
poil de la bête, reprendre du, 73
poil, à, 157
poings fermés, dormir à, 125
poire et le fromage, entre la, 16
poire, se fendre la, 65
Polonais, soûl comme un, 36
pommes, rester dans les, 123
pommes, tomber dans les, 123
pompes, être à l'aise ou *bien dans ses*, 113
pompes, je suis à côté de mes, 111
pompes, je suis mal dans mes, 113
pompes, marcher à côté de ses, 112

pot de peinture sur le visage ou *la tête, on dirait qu'elle ou qu'il a un*, 165
pot, avoir du, 141
pou, moche comme un, 165
pouce, déjeuner sur le, 15
Projet Voltaire, 150
Prometheus, 94
Puce à l'oreille, La, 65

Q

quatre cents coups, faire les, 51
quatre, manger comme , 19
queue de pelle, être rond comme une, 37
qui dort dîne, 29

R

Rabelais, 19, 89
raide dingue de quelqu'un, être, 182
râteau, se prendre un, 187
refus, ce n'est pas de, 14
régime sec, se mettre au, 39
restauration rapide, la, 26
Rey, Alain, 7, 62, 106, 139, 146
rien, je n'y suis pour, 90
rira bien qui rira le dernier, 63
rire jaune, 64
Robert Dictionnaire historique de la langue française, Le, 124, 168, 186
rotules, être sur les, 109
roulettes, marcher (comme) sur des, 53
Rousseau, Jean Jacques, 129

S

SAMU, 93
Sand, George, 124
sang n'a fait qu'un tour, mon, 91
sapeurs-pompiers, 93

sapin, ça sent le, 130
saut, faire le grand, 131
Scholl, Aurélien, 123
sleep, 125-129
sœur ? Et ta, 84
soif, boire à sa, 12
soif, boire jusqu'à plus, 12
soins pour quelqu'un, être aux petits, 181
soleil, lézarder au, 51
souche, dormir comme une, 126
souhaits !, à vos, 94
soupe à la grimace, avoir droit à la, 81
spellings, new rules, 37
Spitting Image, 61
sport, 143-150
St Petersburg, 128
Suppositories, 119

T

tabac, faire un, 52
table ouverte, tenir, 30
Tal, 66
taupe, être myope comme une, 109
terre, c'était à se rouler par, 62
tienne Étienne ! À la, 30, 31, 48
tiennes durent toujours !, Et que les, 94
tire-larigot, à, 45
tomber raide mort, 140
toquer de quelqu'un / quelque chose, (se), 177
tout baigne (dans l'huile), 68
trente et un, se mettre sur son, 167
trou, il/elle boit comme un, 36
Truffaut, François, 52
Tu l'as dit, bouffi !, 48
Tu parles, Charles !, 48
tue-tête, chanter à, 46

U

un(e) de perdu(e), dix de retrouvé(e)s, 189
United Nations, UN, 66

V

Valognes, Aurélie, 88
ver, nu(e) comme un, 166
Verlaine, Paul, 80
verre dans le nez, avoir un, 33
vertes et des pas mûres, en voir des, 83
vie de célibataire, enterrer sa, 180
vie de garçon, enterrer sa, 180
vie de jeune fille, enterrer sa 180
vie en rose, voir la, 55
vin mauvais ou gai ou triste, avoir le, 32
voiture volée, maquillé(e) comme une, 164
Voltaire, 129

W

Wertenbaker, Timberlake, 161
World Happiness Report, 66

Y

yaourt, chanter en, 47
yeux de merlan frit, regarder quelqu'un avec des, 186
yeux en face des trous, ne pas avoir les, 119

Z

Zola, Émile, 129